One
Presentation
Away

Foreword by *New York Times* bestselling author **Amy Porterfield**

One
Presentation
Away

Become an
Irresistible Speaker
and Convert More Clients

Colin Boyd

WILEY

Published by John Wiley & Sons, Inc., Hoboken, New Jersey.
Published simultaneously in Canada.

For general information on our other products and services or for technical support, please contact our Customer Care Department within the United States at (800) 762-2974, outside the United States at (317) 572-3993 or fax (317) 572-4002.

Wiley also publishes its books in a variety of electronic formats. Some content that appears in print may not be available in electronic formats. For more information about Wiley products, visit our web site at www.wiley.com.

Library of Congress Cataloging-in-Publication Data is Available:

ISBN 9781394324316 (Cloth)
ISBN 9781394324231 (ePub)
ISBN 9781394324255 (ePDF)

Cover Design: Wiley
Author Photo: © Griffin Conway

Printed and bound by CPI Group (UK) Ltd, Croydon, CR0 4YY

C9781394324316_181025

The manufacturer's authorized representative according to the EU General Product Safety Regulation is Wiley-VCH GmbH, Boschstr. 12, 69469 Weinheim, Germany, e-mail: Product_Safety@wiley.com.

*For Sarah, thank you for seeing something in me
that I couldn't see in myself.*

Contents

Foreword

The first time I launched a digital course, I made exactly $267. Yep, two hundred and sixty-seven dollars. Not even enough to cover the software I used to sell it.

I had poured my heart into that offer, convinced it would change lives. I mapped out the content, put together the slides, and launched it into the world with so much excitement—only to be met with results that were . . . well, let's just say, humbling.

I remember staring at my screen, refreshing the page, willing more sales to come in. Maybe the emails hadn't gone out correctly. Maybe people needed more time to decide. Maybe—just maybe—the next hour would be different.

But as the launch wrapped up, I faced the hard truth: my belief in my course wasn't enough to sell it. That night, I sat on my couch, replaying every decision I had made.

Was this a sign that I wasn't meant to do this? Had I made the biggest mistake of my career?

That could have been the end of my story. But something in me refused to let this be where it stopped. I wasn't going to let one failed launch define what was possible.

So I went back to the drawing board. I refined my messaging, adjusted my course, and focused on connecting with my audience. I learned how to take what I already knew and present it in a way that truly stuck with people—building not just attention, but lasting trust.

And because of that, my business evolved into something unrecognizable from those early days. I was leading six-figure launches, reaching thousands of people, and creating the kind of impact I once only dreamed about.

But with this growth came new challenges. As I found success in bringing my offers to life through webinars and email, a question emerged:

How do I take this message further?

Beyond the digital walls where my business had been built, where everything felt familiar and safe. Past emails, webinars, and the platforms that were serving me well—but were never meant to be my final stage.

The answer became clearer with every launch. I knew that to create the kind of impact I felt deep in my bones, I had to step into the room and stand on real stages. I had to be there in the energy of the moment, to connect in a way that only happens face-to-face.

But I also knew I couldn't compromise the heart of my business, and I refused to do it in a way that felt scripted, forced, or out of alignment with how I truly wanted to serve.

I needed more than a strategy; I needed a way to carry the magic of what I had built into a new space.

I knew what I wanted. I just didn't know how to make it happen. That's when I went looking for a coach. And that's when I met Colin.

I'll be honest—at first, I was hesitant.

Coaches who help with "influence" and "sales" can sometimes make it all about money and metrics, turning "closing the deal" into a performance.

But Colin was different.

From our very first conversation, I knew he saw sales the way I needed to see it—not as pressure, but as possibility.

And I knew I could trust him because he had walked a similar path.

He had his own story—one of building a course, pouring his heart into it, and then watching it sit untouched, unseen.

But instead of walking away, he got curious. He studied, refined, tested, and uncovered what truly moves people to say yes. And when he figured it out, he didn't keep it to himself—he made it his mission to help others do the same.

That's what drew me to him. Colin had done the work, and in doing so, he didn't just understand the mechanics of selling; he discovered the human side of it. It wasn't about pressure, tactics, or perfectly crafted slide decks. It was about something deeper.

He taught me that selling, at its core, is about creating a moment of clarity for the people you're meant to serve. It's about helping them see, maybe for the first time, that the future they want is possible and that stepping into it isn't just available to them, it's already within them.

So I learned. I listened. I had him coach me through the process.

Then, the day came. The moment I would step onto that stage and put everything I had learned into action. What happened next is something I'll never forget.

As I stood on stage, delivering my presentation, I wasn't worried about getting every word perfect or ensuring my slides were flawless. I wasn't bracing for the moment when I'd present my offer, wondering if people would hesitate or turn away.

I was fully there. Present. Rooted in the belief of what I was saying. And when I presented my offer, I looked into the audience and saw it happen.

The shift. The spark of realization in their eyes. They weren't just listening to me anymore; they saw themselves inside the transformation I offered. They were having a breakthrough.

It was no longer about me.

It was about them stepping into the life they had been waiting for. And one by one, they said yes to my offer.

Working with Colin opened my eyes to what was possible, and I knew I wasn't done. I had seen how the right presentation could spark something in people and how selling wasn't just about delivering information. It was about creating an experience that stayed with them long after the moment had passed.

So as my business grew and multimillion-dollar launches became my new reality, I kept listening—to my audience, to my intuition, to that pull inside me. An undeniable knowing that there was still more to give, more people to serve, and a new way I was meant to show up.

That's when I created a new offer, one that felt different. Bigger. Like the culmination of everything I had learned and everything I wanted to give. This is the kind of work that deserved more than just another launch.

I knew I didn't want this offer to be presented for the first time with an email sequence or webinar pitch. I wanted to be in the room, to witness the moment the people I made this for knew they were stepping forward for the right reasons.

And if I was going to do that, I needed help from the one person I knew could show me how.

So once more, Colin's coaching challenged me, refined me, and elevated my presentation into something more than just words on a stage.

He helped me step fully into the magic of what I was offering, not just as something I believed in but as something my students could feel.

Colin's coaching was part of what helped me sell that offer and build one of the most meaningful things in my life—a thriving community of thousands of students, each inspiring change in ways I never could have imagined.

I think about them often.

The mother who once felt lost in the sleepless haze of early motherhood, now running a multimillion-dollar business, leading other women through that same uncertain season with confidence and grace.

The woman who spent years feeling powerless in her battle with Hashimoto's disease, now using the very method that helped her heal to empower others to take control of their health and reclaim their energy.

The former corporate woman who once navigated boardrooms and tight schedules, now a homesteader carving out a life of simplicity—showing others that a slower, more intentional way of living is possible.

They didn't just build businesses. They created movements.

And they didn't get there by accident.

They learned from me because I had the courage to stand on a stage, share my message, and help them believe in their transformation.

And I could do that because Colin dared to share his message—his coaching, his hard-earned wisdom—so that others like me could step forward and create an even greater impact.

This is how impact multiplies. One act of courage—one moment of stepping forward—creates a ripple effect, opening doors for thousands of people who, in turn, go on to change even more lives.

That's the power of learning to sell from stage as a force for change.

This book, and everything Colin teaches, isn't just about crafting the perfect presentation. It's about stepping forward with your message in a way that doesn't just land in someone's inbox, but lands in their soul.

And if you're reading this, it means you're ready. Ready to step onto the stage. Ready to share what only you can. Ready to turn the knowledge, experience, and passion inside of you into something that moves people to action.

So the real question isn't just about what you'll sell in your presentation.

It's about who will be changed because you dared to stand up and speak.

Because when you create presentations and sell the right way—when you create that moment of clarity—the ripple effect begins. It moves through you, reaches the people you serve, and continues to expand in ways you can't yet see.

And now, with this book in your hands, you have everything you need to create that first ripple.

You really are just one presentation away from everything that's waiting for you—and when you put the teachings in this book into action, you'll spark change in the world in ways you may never fully see but will always be a part of.

—Amy Porterfield, *New York Times* best-selling author

I was sitting at my three-and-a-half-legged wooden desk that I had picked up from the local Goodwill store. One side of the desk was being held up by a pile of books to keep the surface flat. I could hear the train rumbling past our two-bedroom apartment as I sat in my office working on my old laptop.

I was six months into my career of becoming a life coach. I was really excited about the possibilities of this new path ahead. I had huge desires of wanting to build a business where I could coach people and help them reach their potential. My dreams were that this business would give me not only financial reward but a deep sense of meaning in my life. I had seen other people in the industry already starting to do this, but my reality was very different.

I was incredibly frustrated with the fact that my business wasn't moving forward as fast as I wanted. At this point, I basically had no clients and no momentum. Well, I did kind of have a client—I had half a client. It was one of those people you work with where they say they're going to turn up to a coaching session and sometimes they did and sometimes they didn't. Then they pay you every second or third month and keep you hoping that one day it'll turn into a more serious engagement.

To say I was desperate to see a change in my life is an understatement. As I sat at my second-hand desk, my phone rang. It was a friend who was in coaching school with me.

He said he had a speaking engagement coming up that he wasn't able to do. It was a pro bono engagement—in other words, it wasn't paying any money—however, he said it might be a good opportunity for me to get myself out there. I thanked him for the referral and said I would love to do it.

At the time, I was not a professional speaker; the only type of speaking I had done was in college and at my local youth group occasionally on a Friday night in front of 12-year-olds. I remember thinking about this free speaking engagement and starting to freak out completely. I started telling myself: Who do you think you are to speak professionally at an event like this? You're not qualified enough. You're going to get up in front of them, and people are going to think you aren't credible. You're not ready for this type of professional engagement.

I had all of this going through my mind, and I remember having a conversation with my amazing wife, Sarah. She said something to me that changed everything: "It wouldn't have shown up in your life if you weren't ready for it." I decided to believe her and kept on working toward building my presentation for the evening that was inevitably approaching.

When the evening of the event arrived, it was literally a dark and stormy night as I walked up the stairs with my wife on my arm—but in truth, I was really hanging onto her arm. The event organizer saw me and came running over, telling me, "I'm so excited that you came tonight! We are having our biggest event yet—we have 137 people who have come out into the city to hear what you have to say." For me, this was the worst news of the night; not only was I going to get up in front of these people and look stupid, but I was going to do it in front of their biggest crowd to date.

I sat down and nervously waited for the host to introduce me as the speaker for the night. As I got up, I could feel the nerves in my stomach and the sweat on my palms, but despite the fear, I decided to give this my best shot. I did my presentation, and at the end, I made an offer. What I didn't realize at the time was that this offer was an irresistible one. Of the 137 people who were at the event that evening, 125 of them gave me their personal details to follow up about the special offer. My offer was to give a select group of people some free coaching sessions for their career development. This was a beautiful match for the audience as it was a university alumni event.

I diligently followed up and did a lot of consultations in the next week or so. From this follow-up, I ended up signing 12 full-time coaching clients. So in essence, my coaching business went from half a client to 12 after one speaking engagement. Practically overnight, my income went from a few hundred dollars a month to more than $10,000 a month.

About four days after the event, I remember standing on the stairs of a hotel after finishing up with a potential client when my cell phone rang. It was a director from one of the biggest technology companies in the world. He had heard me speak that evening and was sitting in the back corner of the crowd (by the way, you never know who's in the room). He said he loved my presentation and wondered whether I would have any time free over the next couple of months to come and speak at a global training day.

Obviously, I didn't have too much going on, so I told him I'd check my calendar and make sure I was free (which I was!). He asked me how much I would charge to speak at this event. Mind you, I'd never charged a fee before, and I told him it would be $4,500. When I told him that amount, he didn't blink; he said that would be amazing, and they could definitely work with that budget. I was about to find out why he didn't balk at this fee. At the end of the conversation, I asked him how many people would be at this global training day. He said there would probably be between 5 to 5,500 employees. That was the point that I almost died on the phone. But once again, I heard my wife's voice in my mind: "It wouldn't have shown up in your life if you weren't ready for it."

It was from this one experience that I realized the power of speaking. I had been struggling to grow my coaching business using all sorts of methodologies, and one single speaking event completely exploded the possibilities in my life. I took this one truth and started doing this over and over again. I would find events where I could speak at local chapters, I found online communities where I could do webinars and add value, and I put my name forward for various conferences in my area. I went on to build a highly successful and profitable coaching business where we now have more than 10,000 clients around the world, and I get the opportunity to do what I love and get paid handsomely for it.

One Single Presentation Makes the Difference

My revelation from this first professional speaking engagement was that you are just one presentation away from the breakthrough you want in your business. That speaking on a stage, be it in-person or virtual, is the fastest way to build connection, trust, and a stampede of clients for your business. You are closer to your breakthrough than you realize.

The good news gets even better because most people think that you need lots of different types of presentations to have success in your business. The truth is you don't. If you look at a lot of the great speakers and market leaders in your industry, I'll bet that most of them are delivering basically the same presentation wrapped up in different versions over and over again. I've coached people running $10 million per year businesses who literally deliver the same presentation either weekly, monthly, quarterly, or annually. Once you get that single presentation that generates results, you simply need to learn how to grow and scale that presentation in front of more clients to grow your business.

Maybe you are like many of my clients and you are in the expert, coaching, and speaking industry where you help people to see their full potential. Or maybe you're in sales and want to sell technology-based products and other services. I've seen people in so many different industries have ridiculous success by building one high-converting presentation that they deliver over and over again.

I want you to say this with me out loud (if you're worried about looking weird, just put your phone near your ear when you say it): "I am one irresistible presentation away from the breakthrough I want in my business."

Everything starts with the presentation. That is the Holy Grail—you can have the biggest audience in the world, but if you don't have a high-converting presentation that both connects with your audience and moves them toward wanting to work with you, then you're missing the crucial element of your conversion machine. Let's build your presentation so that you can work with your ideal clients and become the market leader in your niche.

What This Book Is About

This book is the definitive guide for entrepreneurs who want to build a high-converting presentation that gets them clients every single time they speak. It is about moving from getting claps to getting a flood of clients. My goal is also to ensure that when you deliver your presentation, it isn't a high-pressure sales presentation. It is something that adds value to all the listeners and results in your audience either inquiring about wanting to work with you or actually buying your program directly at the end of your signature talk.

Who This Book Is For

This book is designed for entrepreneurs and leaders who want to command presence and influence from the stage. It's for people who want to design one powerful presentation that they can deliver over and over again and get clients every single time they speak.

In our business, we have had more than 10,000 people come through our various courses and coaching programs. The majority of those tend to be in the expert industry—for example, they are coaches, course creators, consultants, speakers, or creatives. However, I've also had people in property development, software sales, social selling, and many other industries. As long as you're someone who knows deep down inside your heart that you want to get better at speaking from a stage and getting people to take action, this book will be incredibly useful.

There is a level of vulnerability that everyone experiences when they step on a stage and share their ideas. Speaking from a stage was not something that I initially looked forward to. Some of my earliest memories were feeling incredibly overwhelmed and somewhat traumatized when I was asked to speak or read in front of people. But over the years, I've learned specific strategies that you will discover in this book that have taken me from fearing the stage to loving it.

I've had the privilege to coach thousands of entrepreneurs around the world, and I've had the unique opportunity to advise some of the biggest names in the world. One of the biggest differences I've noticed between those people who are struggling to make progress and the ones who are leading their industry is their courage to try despite their fear. The people you look up to in your industry are human, just like you; they have fears, concerns, and insecurities. But they succeed because they act with courage and not fear. My hope for this book is that it will be more than just another business book you read—it will be a transformational experience that inspires you to play in the big leagues.

Become a Whale

One insecurity I've always had is that I never felt like a leader. I had a certain picture of what a leader was. I thought they needed to be aggressive, demanding, and always speaking up. I never resonated with this idea of that type of leadership so I always held back in considering myself to be a leader. I remember my youth group mentor pulling me aside one day and saying that she noticed I like to be with people who are leaders, but I never stepped in front and led myself. I always stayed in the safety of the pack. I remember a particular event in New York; the workshop room was on the top of a skyscraper in Manhattan. As I looked around the room there were about 30 of us, and there were about 4 people who stood out to me. They were well known and influential in their niche. They were the whales in their industry. As I thought about their skill set, in all honesty, I felt like I was just as good at my craft as they were at theirs. But the difference was that, at the time, I was invisible. I was unknown to the majority of the people in my industry.

That was when a question came into my heart: "What if I became a whale?" What would it take for me to be a market leader? To be someone who is known as a true leader in their expertise? It was at that moment I made a decision to become a whale in my industry. Every day, I started to act as if I was already a market leader. And it was in this decision that my life changed. Within about six months, I had launched my new program Sell From Stage Academy® and had the opportunity to advise some other market leaders on their upcoming presentations and webinars. It was through my decision to choose courage over fear that my life changed.

The fact that you're reading this book I'm assuming means you're someone who loves learning and growing. My encouragement for you today is that you would step into faith instead of fear. That you would feel on a deeper level that responsibility of stepping into your full potential and making the impact you were always called to make. Let's make this journey together.

Part I

The Power of Speaking from the Stage

Chapter 1

How Speaking Will Drive Revenue

As an entrepreneur I've noticed that there are mainly three results that you'll want from your business. The first is income. You cannot escape the fact that if you are in a for-profit business, generating income must be at the top or close to the top of your list. If your business doesn't generate income, you don't have a business—you have an expensive hobby. My experience, through working with thousands of coaches, course creators, and entrepreneurs around the world, is that as much as they genuinely want to make an impact in people's lives, if they aren't making money, making the business sustainable is impossible.

So often, people shy away from the fact that they want to make money. Many people secretly wish they could make more money but don't want to share that publicly because they feel like it's being selfish. I want to give you permission to have an internal drive for income. For me, making money genuinely makes me excited because money represents that the marketplace finds what I am bringing to be valuable.

The second thing people want to create is influence. You probably have a desire in your heart to influence people so that they too can reach their potential. Many of my clients, especially in the expert space, have personally been through a transformation or journey, and they have a desire to influence others so that they too can experience this type of breakthrough.

The final drive for most people is that they want to leave an impact. I tend to attract a lot of heart-centered entrepreneurs, and you are probably one of them. You feel a deep desire to not just make money or a name for yourself but to truly impact people's lives. At the end of most guest episodes on my podcast called *The Expert Edge*, I ask my guests a question that goes something like this: "Imagine it is the end of your life and people are standing around reflecting on what you represented to them. These people are your family, friends, clients, and colleagues. What would be your hope that they would be whispering about you and what you represented in their life?"

Inevitably, almost every time, people speak of the hope that those standing around reflecting on their life would say they made an impact, that they felt loved by them, and that they represented what it looks like to live a life of possibility. I wonder what would be your hope at the end of your life—what would you want people to be whispering about what you represented to them? So often, when I'm delivering a large presentation, I reflect on the idea that when I'm 90 years old, I would love to look back on my life and feel like I represented a path to possibility, that I allowed people to step into their full potential. That is what this book is about for me. The reason I'm writing this is so that when all is said and done, you will always have something available to you that could show you a path to step into your potential. Based on these drives, let's now explore the three pillars for making your speaking business generate high income, have huge influence, and leave a big impact on the world.

Choose Your Audience Wisely

The first pillar of running a successful business is choosing the right audience and knowing them more intimately than they even know themselves. I was about four years into my speaking business and remember going through a period of months when I didn't have much work. Looking at my calendar, I had only one or two speaking engagements, which meant I had a big gap between what I wanted to make that month and what I was actually making.

I opened my email and saw an inquiry from someone asking if I would be willing to speak at one of their conferences. I followed up on the inquiry, and in the discussion, the event organizer shared that they didn't have much of a budget for speakers. When I told them my speaker fee, they said they couldn't afford it but maybe could hire me for a future conference. Remember, I was in a place of desperation, so I said to the event organizer I was willing to do this speaking engagement for half of my regular speaking fee.

When I shared this, he was really excited and said they would love to have me present. I then said to him, "I've recently created an online course that couples beautifully with the presentation I'm delivering. I was wondering if you would be open to sharing that course with the conference in light of me reducing my speaker fee." For context, at this point, I had never sold a product directly from the stage. I had only ever made offers where people could book a free consultation or download some sort of helpful PDF or guide.

The event organizer thought about it for a minute and said that would be great, suggesting we share some of the revenue generated from the course sales as a win-win. We agreed on the concept, and they booked me to present. Leading up to this event, I was really nervous about how this would go. In fact, I thought I'd made a really bad decision to cut my speaker fee because I had no sense of certainty that I would make money from the course offering.

I discussed with the event organizer what I now call a "collaborative close." Essentially, he would come up, congratulate me for the presentation, and then introduce the idea that I had an online course that complemented the presentation. This type of close is really powerful because it takes the pressure off you as the speaker for introducing the course or product.

I had a 30-minute keynote spot. I remember walking on stage and first seeing they'd loaded the wrong slide deck and then noticing the slides weren't showing correctly on the screen. I did all I could to stay calm in front of the audience of about 800 people. I gave the best presentation I could for 30 minutes, and then, at the end, the event organizer came up and started the collaborative close. He thanked me for my time, asked the audience if they found it valuable, and then mentioned my online course that coupled with the presentation content. He passed it to me to share about the course and the special offer for the conference.

I shared details about the course, who it was for, the outcomes, specific modules, and bonuses available, and then shared the special price. I asked the audience members who resonated with my topic to visit a specific URL where they could join the course and get this special offer, available only for people attending the conference in the next 24 hours. The event organizer thanked me again for the presentation; I waved to the audience and stepped off the stage.

As I sat down in the green room, I started to notice a vibration in my pocket. It was my phone, and when I pulled it out, I could see payment notifications showing up on my screen. In complete disbelief, these payment notifications started to come through faster and faster. In the first 10 minutes, about 15 people joined the course; then in the next 30 minutes, about 20 more people joined. Over the next 24 hours, we ended up generating more than $90,000 in course sales. This completely blew my mind. Remember, I had taken this speaking opportunity at a discount rate and was kicking myself for doing that because I hated discounting myself. But what ended up happening was that I made about eight times my regular keynote fee in sales of my online course. This was one of the first times I realized that speaking for a fee was not the best way to generate revenue in my business—it was speaking either for free or for a lower fee with an agreement that I was allowed to make an offer.

To say that I was excited about what had just happened is an understatement. However, I was about to have a rude awakening because several months later, I had an opportunity to speak at an event with a very different audience. I delivered the same presentation to a room of about 250 people. Based on my previous experience, I calculated that I would probably make between $20,000 to $30,000. I did my presentation and made my offer, but this time, I only ended up making $2,000.

I was lost because I didn't understand why; I delivered the same presentation and made the same offer, but I made significantly less money based on the ratio of people present. This was my first lesson in understanding the power of the audience. The audience you choose or end up in front of will determine at least 50% of your success. You can have the most incredible presentation and most irresistible offer, but if you're standing in front of the wrong audience, you'll make very little money. I share this story because who you choose as your audience is one of the most important decisions you'll make as an entrepreneur.

Just recently, I was having a coaching conversation with one of my clients in our group coaching program, and we were discussing that she should elevate her avatar. This meant she should consider focusing on an ideal audience who had more access to resources. I didn't tell her she had to completely abandon her current audience, but we discussed that if she focused more on an audience that had the access and ability to make decisions to join our program, she could make more money. Doing this changed everything because it allowed her to keep her current price and also work with people who had the money to join her program.

Does the audience you're focusing on have the resources to join your program? If you're finding that the offers you're making are extremely inconsistent in how they're selling, it could be an audience problem, not an offer problem. Choose an audience that has the resources and ability to join your program. When you do this, even in economic downturns, they will still have the resources and ability to buy your offerings. These decisions will help you weather economically slow markets and usually result in a better quality experience for you as an entrepreneur because you start attracting more resourceful people.

Develop a Signature Talk

The next element of the equation is building a signature talk that connects with your ideal audience and naturally moves them toward wanting to work with you. Knowing how to structure a presentation that takes your ideal audience on a journey toward greater levels of commitment is the secret to building a high-converting signature talk.

One of the big mistakes people make when building their signature talk is trying to include content that will impress the audience. As human beings, we have a natural desire to be liked. Because of this need, we tend to put content in our presentations that we believe will make the audience think we are either smart, savvy, or successful. The problem with this is that you'll end up creating content that either confuses your audience or overwhelms them with too much information.

Many of the presentations you've attended have probably felt like drinking from a fire hose. It's like going to an all-you-can-eat buffet—at the end, how do you feel? Sick, right? You regret eating so much and feel terrible. A great presentation should feel like an elegant meal. It should be constructed in a way where each idea flows beautifully with the questions or stories you tell. It should have a clear theme and result in the audience feeling fulfilled enough to know they received great information, but not to the point where they feel overwhelmed.

The goal of a presentation that gets you clients is to increase the audience's commitment to the goals they already have. Your presentation should awaken the desires your audience already has for their life and motivate them to take action right now.

One of the problems is that most presentations you have experienced have been information-based, like those from school or college. These presentations are great in an academic environment; however, they are usually emotionally dry in their content, resulting in overwhelm because you're trying to digest too much information. Obviously, I'm generalizing because there are incredible lecturers out there, and I've experienced a few of them, but this is the general experience most of my students describe to me. And it's from this paradigm that most of you will try to create your presentations. You'll focus on cramming in as much content as possible within your allotted time, trying to prove to the audience that you really know what you're talking about. The problem is that in doing so, you're also going to destroy any chances of making a sale.

What tends to happen when you do this is the audience leaves feeling overwhelmed, thinking they have 17 things they need to do before they can even consider joining your program. This happens because you've likely already given them too many action items to tackle.

Ultimately, a presentation that gets you clients should leave your audience with just one action: to take the next step that you offer. Any other action becomes a distraction from them achieving their goal in the fastest way possible, which is through your offer.

Listen carefully because what I'm about to say will change the direction of your life and ideally increase the amount of money you've ever made: a high-converting presentation is designed to help the audience make a decision. The thing most people avoid in their life is making decisions. Decisions are scary because they feel final—they feel like you're cutting off something and heading into a new arena. That's because, on some level, you are. A decision requires you to cut off old ways of thinking, behaving, and acting, and asks you to step into a new way of being.

Essentially, that's what you'll be asking your audience to do. If you make a direct offer, which I call a Sharp Sell, you're asking your audience to make a commitment to change through the offer you're making. This is really scary for your audience because not only are you asking them to make a decision, but you're also asking them to invest in themselves and essentially back themselves to believe they will make a change. The process you're going to take the audience through in your presentation will be touching their hearts, shifting their minds, equipping their hands, and moving their feet. This is the structure that you'll learn throughout this book, and I trust it will change your business and your life.

The great news is that you don't need lots of different signature talks. In fact, I've usually found that most people, including myself, need only one signature talk to get the business breakthrough they've always desired.

Sometimes, we try to get too fancy and come up with new angles and presentations every time we launch the same product. The problem with that is that you're going to get inconsistent results. So, I want you to stop trying to be fancy and start focusing on building one presentation that will get you clients for life. Sometimes people say to me that sounds a little bit boring delivering the same presentation. But can I let you in on a secret? Profitable businesses are usually boring. Profitable businesses are predictable and consistent. If having a pile of cash in the bank, lots of happy customers, and knowing that every time you present, you'll get more clients is boring, I'll take boring every day.

Create an Irresistible Offer

The third pillar you'll need to understand is the power of your offer. Your offer is the program you deliver to help your audience get their desired result. You'll usually make your offer at the end of your presentation. If you do this the right way, you'll get a good percentage of your audience either raising their hands or giving you their credit card details to take the next step excitedly.

Depending on the context, you'll either be:

- Asking your audience to sign up directly and join your paid offer
- Inviting them to book a call with you or your team members to discuss their situation and if they are a good fit for the next step
- Offering a free resource like a PDF, guide, or training in exchange for their personal details

As a rule of thumb, you should always ask permission from the event organizer to make an offer. Obviously, if you're hosting your own presentation for your own audience, you have complete freedom to make whatever offer you desire. That type of situation is my favorite because it gives you full freedom. But if you're speaking at an event that is a collaboration of other people's audiences or you've been invited to present at someone else's conference, you must always ask permission. Your offer should be the logical next step after hearing your signature presentation and should align directly with your ideal audience's existing desires.

The secret to building a highly profitable business is finding an audience you like working with and who can afford to pay you, building a signature talk that naturally moves them toward wanting to take up your offer. Your offer should deliver on its promises, which will result in goodwill, great reviews, and consistent referrals. This synergy of your audience, signature talk, and offer will create momentum like you've never experienced before.

Chapter 2

The Power of the Stage

As a business owner, you have a strong desire to be known in the market, respected for your expertise, and in a position where your audience asks to work with you and your services.

For most business owners, the opposite is true—their products are unknown, the products are not yet desired, and it feels like they have to do everything under the sun to get a single sale.

That's where the power of the stage comes in. What most people don't realize about the stage is that it has superpowers.

The Three Superpowers of the Stage

When you step on stage, you transition from being Clark Kent to being Superman. There are built-in assumptions that the stage brings to the minds and hearts of your audience that allow you to become more attractive and desirable to work with.

Authority

The first superpower of the stage is that it gives you authority. The fact that you are the one standing on the stage in front of them means you are in an elevated position compared to everyone else in the room. There is a built-in assumption that if you are on the stage, you know what you're talking about, you wouldn't be there if you weren't trusted already, and you are confident as a person. These are specific things that your audience is looking for in relation to solving their problems. I believe authority is probably the most important factor when it comes to building trust fast with a cold or warm prospect.

Connection

The second superpower of the stage is that it creates connection. It's great to be an authority in your market, but if you can't show your prospects that you understand them and connect with them, then there will be a disconnect between you and them. Connection is the second superpower that enables the stage to speed up the time between curiosity and becoming a client. The reason why connection occurs so fast on a stage is that your audience can visually see you, verbally hear you, and emotionally connect with you. Even if you're presenting on a virtual stage like a webinar or an online event, the connection you have with your audience is elevated because they can visually see how you move, how you act, and how you interact with them. The speed at which trust is transferred and created when they can feel your feelings, hear the tone in your voice, and see how you look is dramatically increased. Your audience is asking the question, "Do I connect with you?" They're wondering if they connect with you as a speaker and presenter. They're looking for leadership in their life; however, they also want to feel connected to you.

Leverage

The third superpower of the stage is leverage. I love going to networking events; as a people person, I really enjoy connecting with new people and having conversations one-on-one over a few snacks and drinks. However, the problem is that at a networking event, I can speak to only 5–20 people maximum. Sure, the power of this is immense because you create deep connections, and they could lead to more business in the future. The problem with this is that it's very limited.

When you're speaking on a stage, the leverage of one-to-many is so powerful. Whether you're hosting an in-person event or a virtual event, the fact that you get 30–60 minutes of the entire audience's time while you share your ideas and win them over (and ideally work with them in the future) gives you an advantage that no one else in the room has. As a business owner, if you want to grow your business, having one-on-one sales conversations is a great way to understand your prospects and to sell your services. The problem with it is that it's exhausting and, once again, very limited. I had been attending networking events early on in my business for years—I built some great relationships and got a few referrals here and there, but I hadn't built a viable business. It was amazing to see that in one presentation, my business went from just a few clients to a whole load of coaching clients.

The power of this is in the combination of these three superpowers. It's through the synchronicity of having authority, connection, and leverage that moves you into a superhuman status. You're no longer like everyone else in the room; you're instantly the go-to person. If you present in the right way, you become the one person in the room that everyone wants to talk to and work with.

Defining the Stage

It's important now to define a stage. A stage is any platform where people can visually see you, verbally hear you, and emotionally connect with you in a one-to-many format. When considering these three modalities, you can quickly see that there are many types of stages.

To have a clear definition of a stage for the purpose of this conversation, I'm really talking about a platform where a group of people can see, hear, and feel your presence for a set period of time, where you are the main person they are listening to and connecting with.

In my mind, I categorize stages in two main areas: in-person stages and virtual stages. Let's look at these next.

In-Person Stages

Some examples of in-person stages are when you are speaking at an in-person event. Maybe you are doing a presentation, hosting a workshop, delivering a seminar, or facilitating a brainstorming session. These are all different versions of an in-person stage. Essentially, it's where you are speaking to the whole room and leading the room to a result.

You don't have to be the main keynote speaker at a conference; you could be a breakout speaker. These also don't have to be huge events—they could be small local events that you're hosting in your area with 5–10 people attending. The secret is that you are speaking to more than one person, and you are the designated speaker for that period of time.

Many people think that the goal of being a speaker is to be paid to speak. Sure, being paid to speak is great, but running your own events is just as powerful, if not better. The reason for this is that if you're hosting your own event, not only can you make money on ticket sales but you have full permission to make any type of offer to the audience. A lot of the time, when you are paid to speak or you're speaking on someone else's stage, there are restrictions around what you can offer the audience as a next step.

Virtual Stages

I've been using virtual stages for more than a decade, well before they became popular during the pandemic. I think through that period of time, they accelerated in their practicality and acceptability. I believe this is a great thing because the reach that you can get from a virtual stage, based on the cost of hosting the event, gives it lots of advantages.

I don't believe that a virtual event replaces an in-person event, but I do believe that a lot of the time, the advantages as the host outweigh the disadvantages. And for many people, it's really convenient to not have to get on a plane and fly across the country to connect with you and hear your presentation.

Virtual stages include webinars, a range of virtual events, and live video series.

Webinar

A webinar is one of the most controlled virtual environments. This is where you, as the speaker, are delivering a presentation, and the audience cannot really see or interact with each other. Think of this as the classic teacher or classroom setting. All the students are facing the front, listening to the teacher. The webinar is fairly well known in the industry and fantastic for delivering a high-value sales presentation that runs between 60 to 120 minutes for audience sizes from 10 to 10,000+ attendees.

Virtual Events

Virtual events can be used for many purposes, but the big factor that you'll want to consider is their scope. Typically, virtual events can be a day or less, multiday events, or full-blown summits.

Half- or Full-Day Virtual Events

I've run dozens of these where for anywhere between two and six hours per day, you'll be delivering content and getting the audience to experience practical exercises throughout the day. If you're hosting longer virtual events, it's really important to increase engagement throughout the experience. A 60-minute presentation is fine without too many practical exercises, but as soon as you get to two hours and longer, not only do you need practical exercises for the audience, I even recommend using breakout rooms where the audience can get to know other people in the event. More on this later.

Multiday Virtual Events

Multiday virtual events are similar to a half- or full-day virtual event, but essentially you're taking your audience through a journey over multiple days. This can work great if you're doing a deep transformational experience with your audience and you have an offer that is at a price point of $3,000 or more. Multiday events are fantastic because they build even greater trust with your audience, and therefore conversion rates into your offers will increase dramatically. Personally, I really like two-day virtual events; I find that after two days, sometimes the attendance can drop, especially if you're doing multiple hours per day.

Virtual Summit

Summits are great experiences as a virtual event because you usually get a series of different speakers over multiple days. The audience can experience lots of different topics and content. The advantage of this is that because you involve lots of different presenters and speakers, it can sometimes be easier to get registrations for these events, especially if you're delivering to the general public. You'll also get greater reach because the speakers for the event will usually promote that they are speaking at the summit to their audiences.

The disadvantage of running summits is that they're not the greatest mechanism to sell your products, courses, or coaching. This is because there are so many topics and different speakers that can dilute the power of the main message. For me, running summits with multiple speakers is more of an audience-building exercise than it is a sales mechanism. A lot of my clients have had great success, including myself, either hosting or speaking at summits. It gives you great exposure to new audiences and allows you to build credibility in your marketplace as you are one of the featured speakers at the summit.

Live Video Series

A multipart video series is one of my favorite ways to launch products and services. Essentially, this structure is where you're delivering anywhere between three to four videos, preferably live, so the audience can interact with you. Over these multiple videos, you're building beliefs, desires, and concepts that move your audience toward buying into your offer. In this style of delivery, you want to ensure there is lots of value through-out the presentations, which builds tremendous trust with your audience. This video style is usually 60–90 minutes per pres-entation delivered over three to four days. I'll usually make an offer on the third or fourth video to give people time to make a decision as to whether to move forward or not.

Webinar vs. Meeting Formats

One important distinction is to understand the difference between meetings and webinar formats. The advantage of host-ing your virtual presentation as a webinar is that you have a lot more control over the experience. A webinar is where essen-tially you are the main focus of the presentation. The audience cannot see each other; however, depending on the settings, they can comment and interact with each other. Think about this as a classroom experience—everyone is sitting forward, facing you as the virtual presenter and not really interacting with each other. This is great for a presentation anywhere between one and two hours. For anything longer than this, I usually prefer a meeting format.

Meeting formats are really useful if you're trying to create more intimacy and interaction within the presentation. I like to use meeting formats for virtual events where I want more inter-action with the audience members. I host a regular two-hour event where I teach storytelling; instead of hosting this in the webinar format, I host it in a meeting format. This allows me to split up the audience into breakout rooms so that they can share their experiences with other members.

There's something magical that happens when audience members get to connect with each other and talk about the concepts you're teaching. From a learning perspective, it integrates with them on a deeper level, but it also connects them with the group. From my experience, the greater engagement you can get with your audience, the higher the conversion rate into your offers will be. So, if you're running virtual events and you're getting fewer than 100 people showing up to these events, I personally like hosting them in a meeting format. You'll get more intimacy with your audience; however, you need to be conscious of controlling the meeting, especially if the audience you're inviting are new to you, in other words, they aren't clients yet.

The Power of a Presentation Quadrant

Finally, let's understand how speaking on a stage has advantages over other selling methodologies through the power of a presentation quadrant.

There are two spectrums to consider when growing your sales:

- The first spectrum is the number of people who will say yes to your products and services. This is referred to as the *conversion rate*—in other words, the percentage of people who hear what you have to say and say yes to taking the next step.
- The second spectrum is leverage, in other words, how many people will see the content or presentation.

If we lay this out in a 2 × 2 quadrant, you can see four ways of selling your services. (See Figure 2.1.)

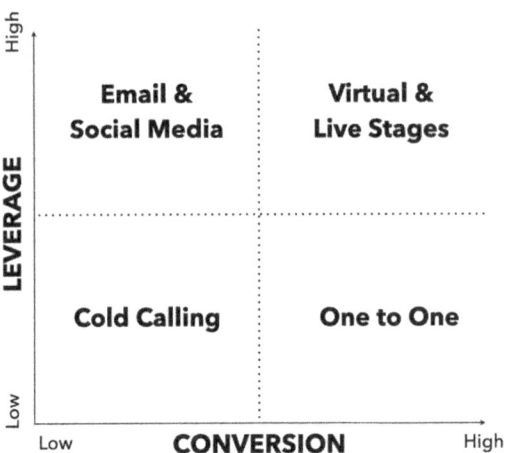

Figure 2.1 Showing the power of a presentation quadrant

One-to-One Selling

One-to-one selling usually gives you a high conversion rate. If you have qualified prospects in front of you, selling one-to-one is an extremely powerful way to convert them into your programs.

The challenge with this approach is that it can be incredibly time-consuming. If you're doing the one-to-one selling yourself, not only do you need to qualify your prospects (usually with a short conversation or survey), but you also have to spend your time with each prospect, hoping they will say yes. It's normal for sales calls to go for 30–60 minutes, and if it's not done right, the prospect often says, "Let me think about it."

Social Media and Email Marketing

The second and popular way of selling is through social media or email. The advantage of social media is that you have extreme leverage. Depending on the size of your database or the reach and engagement that you have on your social platforms, you can reach thousands of people.

The problem, however, is that you will get a low conversion rate into your programs. I've had many clients come to me prior to using the methods you're learning in this book and say they have launched products and services through social media and email with very poor results. They had high expectations that they were going to get hundreds of sales but ended up with one or two. It's normal to get less than 1% conversion rate from your database into your offers. Obviously, this depends on how much engagement and the level of value you've been giving your audience prior to releasing your programs.

Cold Calling and Cold Messaging

The third way of trying to sell your services is through cold calling and cold messaging. Let's be frank, no one likes cold calling (as much as the people who teach cold calling say that it can be really enjoyable), and the results are really poor. I'm approached by hundreds of people cold calling every single week, whether through social media or via email, and I've never said yes to anyone. The problem with cold calling is that the prospects you're trying to reach out to are exactly what it's called—*cold*—and warming them up is a difficult process, especially if you are the uninvited guest.

The Magic of Virtual and Live Stages

This leaves us with why using virtual and in-person presentations are the most effective way to get a flood of new clients into your business. The magic of this is that doing a presentation incorporates both of the two most important spectrums in sales:

- It provides you with the mechanism for leverage—your presentation is delivered one-to-many. This might be a small crowd when you first start out, but it will get bigger as you learn the methodologies in this book.
- It provides you with a high conversion rate. When you present in a way that creates an irresistible desire for people wanting to work with you and you combine the superpowers of the stage (authority, connection, and leverage), you end up with incredible conversion results.

Virtual presentations will usually have a slightly lower conversion rate than in-person presentations; however, there are incredible advantages to hosting virtual presentations as opposed to in-person. I love both, but I think that when you're getting started in your business, focusing on virtual stages is probably the most cost-effective and easiest way to get started.

As you can see from the presentation quadrant, speaking to an audience provides the advantages of leverage and high conversion rates. This will result in you getting a flood of clients into your business without needing to build a massive database, make uncomfortable cold calls, or have endless one-to-one conversations with prospects.

Part II

Establishing Yourself and What You Offer

Chapter 3

Unlock Your Confidence

I was sitting in class as a 13-year-old boy, waiting for my turn to read aloud in front of the class. I had high socks on, gray shorts, and my blue and yellow tie. As I nervously waited and heard each of my classmates read a few paragraphs, I started to get anxious. It was coming closer and closer to me, and soon it would be my turn.

My classmate beside me finished his reading, and now the crucial moment had begun. I started to read my paragraph and, all of a sudden, froze up. I began to stutter over the words, and it almost felt like I had forgotten how to read. Then, my eyes started to go blurry, and I began to experience a level of tunnel vision that stopped me from seeing the words in front of me. I tried to keep pushing through as I didn't want to look stupid in front of the entire class. What was weird was that I had been reading for years—it was something I could do—but for some reason, I couldn't do it in front of the class. About halfway through the paragraph, I stopped reading, took a breath, and then tried as hard as I could to finish the last few sentences. When I finished, it moved on to the next kid in the class, and I sat through the rest of that lesson mulling over what had just happened.

As I walked out of that classroom, I remember thinking, "What is wrong with me? Everyone else in the class can read fluently, and I'm the only one who really struggled with that exercise."

Creating Meaning

From that experience, because I couldn't read in public, I decided I must be stupid. It was a catalyst for the next decade of my life, and I couldn't shake that belief. I found myself in situations and circumstances at work, at school, and with friends where I would interpret situations to mean, "This is happening because I'm an idiot." But how I felt in those moments and the meaning that I attached to myself was my own creation.

Obviously, this belief was not something that served and supported me in my confidence. But to be honest, I had no idea that it was a belief I had about myself until I started to understand personal development.

This experience formed a deep fear in me about speaking in public. When I was in college, I was asked to do a three-minute presentation in front of my class for a marketing subject we were studying. That three minutes felt like three hours. As I stood in front of the class, I remember my hand starting to shake as I was holding my notes. And as I could see my hand shaking, I tried to grab my notes with my other hand, and then that started shaking. Then I grabbed my notes with both hands and then they both started shaking. Then my knee started shaking. I felt like I was having an all-out panic attack standing in front of the class while everyone was looking at me.

I think many of us have had some traumatic experiences when it comes to speaking in public. There is a reason why it's sometimes referred to as the one fear that is greater than the fear of death. When you're standing in front of an audience, there's a vulnerability that you don't experience in everyday life. If you have the wrong mindset about it, you feel very exposed, almost like everyone is watching you and waiting for you to fail.

That's definitely how I felt about public speaking. It's amazing now to think that my full-time business is teaching people to speak persuasively in public.

I share this story because I want you to know that if you currently have a fear of speaking in public, there is a solution. You're about to discover some key ideas that have transformed the way that I feel about standing in front of an audience.

But one thing I want to note here is that this book is so much bigger than speaking in public—it's about learning to sell from a stage. On one level, this is an even more daunting task; not only must you move past your fear of speaking in public, but you must also learn to feel comfortable selling. My goal is to address both of these resistances in this chapter. There is a way to access a greater level of confidence when you speak in public, and there is a clear path for learning how to feel comfortable selling your products and services, without feeling pushy or salesy.

Reframing Your Meaning

At the age of 26, I discovered personal development. I signed up for a life coaching program that fundamentally changed the way I saw the world. During one of the classes, the facilitator shared the idea that "the map is not the territory." This is a concept that comes from the study of neuro-linguistic programming (NLP), and it means the way you see yourself and the reality of the world is different. Essentially, how you see yourself is the map, and the territory is the true reality or the facts. You interpret the facts through your perception, which creates your own unique map. The problem is that your map is never the true territory. It is simply your interpretation of how you saw the events. The wild thing is that in almost every circumstance, each person has a different interpretation of what the facts mean, even when they experience the same event. Recognizing this is empowering because it allows you permission to examine the meaning that you've created from experiences you've had.

If we go back to my experience in school as a young boy, the way I saw the events was because I struggled to read in front of my classmates meant that "I was an idiot." Now, my hope is that when you picked up this book and saw the title, you didn't think, "I'm really looking forward to reading this book because the author seems like an idiot." (I hope that wasn't the case!)

Just as I learned to reconsider the way I saw events, I want you to be able to reconsider how your life experiences have shaped your beliefs about yourself and about speaking and selling in front of an audience. These beliefs are either helping or hindering you from reaching your full potential.

The good news is that the meanings you've created from your experiences are malleable. In other words, when you become aware of these meanings and reframe them in a more empowering way, you'll not only feel better about speaking but also be able to act with greater confidence.

These are some of the typical limiting beliefs I've noticed among my students:

- "I'm not enough of an expert."
- "I'm not good enough."
- "I'll be judged."
- "No one will buy my program."
- "Selling is too uncomfortable for me."

- "I'm not a great storyteller."
- "I'm just not good at speaking in public."

Every single one of these is a belief we've created. We form these beliefs based on evidence gathered from our experiences. The problem is that these beliefs are distorted by thousands of other experiences from our upbringing.

I'd love to take you through a powerful process to identify your limiting beliefs and realign them with a more empowering identity.

Identifying Your Beliefs

Take a moment and ask yourself: "What do I believe about my ability to speak and sell in front of an audience?" Imagine if I told you that 3,000 people were coming to a conference where you were the main speaker, and you were invited to pitch your product from the stage. How would you feel? For most people, this would trigger a blend of excitement, anxiety, and overwhelm.

Imagine approaching this critical presentation in your life— what things do you tell yourself about your ability to succeed? The answer isn't about impressing me or anyone else; it's about finding the truth. Business coach and author Dan Sullivan has a great quote: "All progress starts by telling the truth." When you start with the truth about what you believe about yourself and how you show up in the world, it helps you build a solid foundation for more empowering beliefs.

If you don't start by understanding what you're currently telling yourself, it's like putting whipped cream on a dead raccoon (excuse the visual). So the first part of this process is basically identifying the negative thoughts lying around in your brain. For me, my original beliefs were as follows: "I am an idiot," "I'm terrible at speaking in public," "When I stand in front of an audience, I shake," and "I'm too young to be credible." If I'm really honest, these were the beliefs I had about myself when I first started as a coach. But recognizing that I held these beliefs enabled me to start reframing them and create more empowering ones.

The first new belief I created about myself was "I'm an intelligent, proactive, enthusiastic individual." It's quite a mouthful when I look back on it now, but it set me up for reframing my beliefs about myself. The challenge is that at this phase, you look around yourself and think, "Where is the evidence to support this new identity?" You might initially find very little proof to support this new identity; however, as you start declaring it over your life and to yourself continually, you'll notice more and more evidence to support this new experience of the world.

For me, I love to physically write out these new beliefs. Each morning, especially when I'm going through a transformational period in my life and business, I will literally write out my new beliefs. Some of the other beliefs I'd adopted throughout this process are "I'm a transformational coach," "I'm a world-class trainer and speaker," and "When I step on stage, I freaking rock."

But I'll tell you the truth: when I started declaring these beliefs about myself, I had very little evidence. I didn't rock on stage, I wasn't a transformational coach, and I wasn't a world-class trainer and speaker. But it started with deciding that I was, and after deciding that, I started to find little bits of evidence that supported this new belief.

Building Your Evidence

I was standing on the stairs of a hotel after just delivering a one-on-one coaching session with a new prospect who had signed up for my coaching package. I was feeling exhilarated about how things were starting to build with my business when I felt a vibration in my pocket. I pulled my phone out and answered the unknown number. The man on the other line said that he was an audience member from one of the presentations I had delivered several weeks back. He was calling from a major technology company and was wondering if I would be available to speak at one of their global finance training days in a few months. I said I would need to check my calendar (but to be honest, I was just saying this to make it sound like I was in demand—I knew I was available!). After a quick check of the calendar, I came back to him and said, "Yes, I'm free that day." He asked me what my speaking fee for the event would be.

The problem was I'd never charged for speaking. I had no idea what I should say other than an amount that my mentor had said they started delivering keynotes at. I nervously told him the amount, which was $4,500, and instantly, he came back and said, "That's definitely within the budget—let's move this forward." I was really taken aback that he said yes so quickly to my amount, and I was about to find out why. Keep in mind that this was the first sales call I'd ever had regarding selling my speaking, and as a rookie move, the last question was probably one of the most important questions that I should have asked before I even shared my price. As we were closing out the conversation, I asked, "How many people will be attending this global training day?" His answer was, "There should be anywhere between five to five-and-a-half-thousand people."

My world went all fuzzy at this moment, thinking about the fact that I was about to deliver my first paid presentation to a Fortune 500 company with 5,500 people in attendance. Before this presentation, I had very little evidence that I was a speaker someone would pay money for, let alone give the responsibility of inspiring 5,500 people at one event. The only time I'd spoken was at college, my youth group, and one free presentation as a coach.

But I had been working on my beliefs and declaring the fact that I was a world-class trainer and speaker, a transformational coach, and an intelligent, proactive, enthusiastic individual— someone who rocked the stage. I truly believe that it was that declaration, which started months before this invitation, that attracted this opportunity into my life.

Now, I'd like to share with you a few empowering beliefs and mindset shifts that I believe every entrepreneur must make in order to speak with confidence and sell their products and programs with certainty.

Selling Is Serving

You probably feel, like most people, at least a little internal resistance when it comes to selling. This usually occurs because you've had some bad experiences of being sold to. Maybe you bought a product or a program that you felt pressured into buying, and after purchasing it, you regretted the decision. I think there is a stigma when it comes to selling because we really don't want to be a salesy or pushy person. The problem is that in avoiding trying to be pushy, you'll avoid growing your business and selling your products.

But there is a way in which you can offer your products and services so that it feels good and not pushy, which we will explore throughout this book. However, before we get into the tactical side of things, there must be a shift philosophically. Unless you view selling as serving, you'll always experience internal resistance. This means fewer people will join your programs, you'll make less money, and you'll impact fewer lives.

I believe selling is deeply understanding your audience and communicating in a way whereby the right people are naturally drawn to commit to themselves on a higher level through your offer. When selling is done right, it is an incredibly honoring, respectful, and empathetic process. It also allows you to provide a solution to someone who may not have found that solution elsewhere. So let's explore how you can start to see selling as serving because when you view it as a part of your service, it will feel so much more congruent, easy, and exciting. Let's shift this belief right now.

The truth is that you have two groups of people in your business. You have a group of people who are prospects—they see your posts on social media, interact with your emails, and watch your YouTube channel. Let's call these people "outside your offer." Then there is a second group who have bought something from you—they are clients who have paid you money and are moving through a transformation experience that your product or program provides. Let's call this group "clients."

From these two groups, where do you get the greatest transformations or testimonials? This isn't a trick question. Ideally, the answer is the people who are clients. So in other words, as much as you can provide a transformational experience for people who are consuming your free content, the highest level of transformation is experienced by people who have paid you money and become clients. In other words, when you sell and people buy, you are able to serve them and their goals in life on a higher level. I would even go so far as to say that selling is serving at an even higher level.

Many people associate serving with doing something for someone, expecting nothing in return. As much as this is a great idea, from a commercial business perspective, this is not how capitalism and entrepreneurial societies work. In fact, I think it's really unhealthy if this is the perspective you take in your business. So, when I'm talking about the idea of serving, I'm referring to helping the client reach their goal faster, easier, and with less pain. I'm not talking about serving at a soup kitchen with homeless people—although this is a really noble task, it's probably not your core business. So, in the context of your business, serving is providing an integrated solution to your audience's problems. And if you do this the right way, you'll gain an incredible reputation in the market, and your clients will come up to you and thank you for creating a program that, inevitably, they paid for.

I was hosting a live event recently, and one of my clients came up to me. I could sense a bit of hesitation in her voice, and she said to me, "Can I share something with you privately that I haven't shared publicly with you?" I felt a little bit nervous but accepted. She looked me straight in the eye, and I could see that she was misting up a little. (I thought, "Oh great, now I'm making people cry—this is definitely not going to be good.") She went on to say that prior to meeting me and using my business strategies, she had been making between $10,000 to $15,000 per month, which was good but didn't allow her to live and provide for her family in the way that she wanted. She said that she recently hit an average of $80,000 per month and was able to buy a new house, go on a family vacation she'd always wanted with her kids, and build a team that supports her in her business. She said, "I want you to know this would not have been possible without your direction, strategies, and help. You've literally changed the quality of my life and my kids' lives, thank you."

It's these sorts of moments that remind me of the very reason why I am a coach. This is why I started my business in the first place: to truly make an impact in people's lives and to help serve their goals so that they can create the life and experience the full potential that they have always dreamed of.

Let's reflect on your life now. I want you to think about a program, course, book, or coaching experience that you've had where you paid money to experience it and it truly made a positive impact on your life. As you think about that experience, I want you to consider what would have happened if the creator of that resource had decided that they felt too uncomfortable to make this offer—that they decided they didn't want to come off as salesy and pushy, and so they ended up avoiding releasing this incredible resource to the world and to you. What would be missing in your life if this occurred? I know for me there are programs, books, and experiences that, when I look back on them, were defining points in me growing my business and experiencing life at a greater level.

Now, I want you to brace yourself because here is the kicker: you are that person for your audience. In other words, if you don't see selling as serving and you instead hold back your offers, there will be people in this world who won't experience the fullness of their potential because you decided not to offer it. The truth is I can't be that person for your audience; only you can. I have a specialized skill that sees a specific result, and so do you. You have people in your audience that I will never help or impact—it is your mission and responsibility to build experiences whereby they get to grow, develop, and become all they're called to be. Your selling becomes your serving.

Stop Reading and Start Connecting

I'm sitting on a wooden chair, intently watching my 11-year-old son deliver his presentation to me in preparation for his classroom delivery. He'd been asked by his teacher to present a short speech about American history. He tells me, "Dad, everyone in the class just stands in front and reads from the paper to the class. Should I just do that?" This is where Super Dad comes in and says no son of mine will be reading for their speech. After a few practices, his confidence grew dramatically, and he's now checking his notes only two or three times for the entire presentation. He's let go of the need to say the right words and embraced a willingness to connect with me as his audience. I watch his confidence transform as he stops reading and starts connecting.

The problem is most of us grow up thinking that a speech is essentially reading from slides. This is so boring for the audience and takes all the life out of the delivery. Have you ever had a death-by-presentation experience? You're sitting in the audience, and the presenter is literally reading word for word off the slide. In your mind, you're thinking, "Why don't you just send me these slides and I'll read through them in half the time and save the next hour of my life from this drudgery?" Reading from slides isn't a presentation—it's a reading. This is fine if you're reading your child a book; it's not fine if you're delivering a dynamic presentation to prospects who are looking to engage your services.

I want you to stop seeing a presentation as a presentation and start seeing it as a conversation. The idea of a conversation is that it's a two-way experience, and as much as a speech has 90% one-way delivery (i.e., the speaker to the audience), when you change your thinking and start viewing it as simply having a conversation with the audience, you'll approach the delivery in a totally different energetic space.

I even like to start a presentation by saying, "As we have this conversation today." It sets a frame that we are in a conversation, and even though it is very much one-way, I want the audience to feel like it's two-way. And the truth is, it is two-way because even if audience members don't share, they're also having a conversation with themselves in their own heads about the things you're talking to them about. So there is a level of two-way conversation happening.

Make the goal of your presentation to connect, influence, and empower, as opposed to just getting the right information across to the audience.

No One Knows What You Were Supposed to Say

Delivering a presentation can be quite a vulnerable experience because you're standing in front of a group of people while everyone's looking at you. Nobody wants to look stupid in front of other people. The problem with this is that we get into a perfectionist pattern. You start thinking that you have to get everything right. But here's a little secret that I want you to put in your back pocket: no one knows what you are supposed to say. This one idea can completely set you free from perfectionism in your speaking. Unless someone has the exact word-for-word script that you're following (which I don't ever recommend anyway), no one in the audience will even know if you are saying the right thing or not.

I've had many times delivering a 60-minute presentation where I have completely forgotten key stories, metaphors, and examples, or even just left them out due to time constraints, and I have never had someone come up to me and say, "I think you missed a key story in your presentation." This hasn't happened to me in more than 16 years of speaking and literally thousands of presentations. If it hasn't happened to me yet, I want to encourage you not to worry about it either. Let go of the need to be right and thinking that there is a perfect way of delivering something, and realize that no one knows what you were supposed to say.

Obviously, your presentation needs to make sense, be emotionally and intellectually engaging, and move them toward an outcome, but as long as it does that, there's no right or wrong.

Get It in Your Body

Have you ever been standing in front of an audience about to deliver a presentation, and you can't find the words to describe what you're trying to say? Have you ever felt like you've been really clear in your head, and you go to share it, and it comes out nothing like you thought it would? This usually occurs because you haven't got the speech in your body. One of my recommendations when preparing for the delivery of your presentation is to deliver your speech out loud at least 5 or even 10 times. You have to connect your brain to your mouth. When you deliver your speech out loud in combination with your slides or whatever delivery tools you're using, it gets the content into your body.

When you first start designing a presentation, you're actually dealing with a lot of chunks of information. These chunks of information include your content, stories, body movement, PowerPoint presentation, audience interaction, and breathing. The goal is to practice your presentation to a point where these five or six chunks of information start to integrate into smaller chunks. If you do this during preparation, on the day of your presentation delivery, your unconscious mind has integrated a lot of these separate parts of information so that the content comes out of your mouth with more fluency and flow. You'll be able to interact with the audience and respond to their questions, reactions, and energy so much easier when you've practiced the presentation and got it into your body.

I personally love to practice in front of a mirror. I'll deliver my presentation and allow myself to make lots of mistakes. It's really funny because I actually feel nervous presenting to myself in front of a mirror. It feels really awkward the first couple of times, but after some perseverance, my confidence starts to build in the delivery. This also allows a lot of the nervous energy to run through my body so that on the day of delivery, I'm not carrying that energetic load into the presentation. I'll have space to deliver with presence and power.

For you to develop the confidence to both speak and sell during a presentation, you must build empowering beliefs that serve and support you. Even if you find speaking incredibly scary, there is a path you can take to completely redefine your confidence and delivery. But it all starts in your mind—it starts from identifying and rebuilding how you view speaking and selling. The ideas in this chapter will help to lay a foundation for you to go from freaked out to all-out confidence.

Chapter 4

The Core Premise

Your core premise is one of the most important parts of your presentation. It forms the backbone of the message you will build throughout your presentation. In reviewing thousands of presentations over the years, I rarely see people have a clear core premise within their presentation. This leads to confusion, overwhelm, and a lack of results. I don't want this to be the experience that you have, so let's get this sorted for you.

Think of your core premise as the single most important belief that you must transfer to the audience for them to want to work with you. It is the through-line that links your presentation to your offer. To show you the importance of this, I remember a student of mine, Tiyana, who came to me at a level where she had already established some success in her business.

She had built a business where she was running webinars producing around $30,000 in revenue per presentation, but she knew she had something bigger and deeper within her. Her feedback to me was that discovering her core premise gave her a clarity and confidence to market the business like never before. Through this clarity, she was able to design her presentations more effectively. From there, she went from doing $30,000 virtual presentations to delivering her next presentation for $148,000, and then she delivered a presentation that resulted in $298,000 of revenue.

What's now great to see is how Tiyana leveraged this core premise even beyond her presentations. The same message that transformed her webinars became the foundation for her software-as-a-service (SaaS) company, BeautyPro Funnels, which is an all-in-one business management software for independent beauty professionals. She's been able to transcend using her core message for presentations into launching an entirely new technology solution that serves her market. The exciting thing was that it took one only clear core premise to create these multiple breakthroughs, proving that when you have clarity in your message, it can scale across different business models and platforms.

The Single Sentence That Matters

Your core premise will essentially be made up of a single sentence. This single sentence describes a belief that your audience must understand and accept in order to see your offer as the logical next step.

My core premise is: you are one irresistible presentation away from the breakthrough you want in your business.

Essentially what I'm saying is that through building an irresistible presentation, you'll get the confidence and ability to attract more clients. This concept is the most important idea I must get across when delivering a presentation. In fact, this idea is the foundation for my entire business. Essentially, I help people build presentations that get them clients. So if you are a prospect coming to me initially and you hear me share that sentence—that all you need is one irresistible presentation and your business can explode—then you understand what I do and how I get you a result.

You need that sentence for your business. You need a sentence that clearly articulates what you do and the result you get people.

Another way of describing your core premise is stating the vehicle and then stating the result.

For example, I could say: "Building an irresistible presentation is the fastest way to get a breakthrough in your business." If you take a look at the sentence structure, essentially what I'm doing is saying that if you use the vehicle of a presentation, then you'll get the result of a business breakthrough. This will make more sense as you understand what a vehicle and a result will look like.

So, let's dive even deeper into the anatomy of a core premise and how you create one yourself. As I mentioned, a core premise comprises two main things: a vehicle and a result.

The Four Vehicles

I've studied the marketplace for many years, and I've noticed there are four types of vehicles you can choose from. In the following sections, I'll take you through each of the four vehicles, and essentially, you're going to choose one of them to use in your core premise.

The Thing Vehicle

A thing vehicle is a type of vehicle whereby you help your clients achieve a result through a thing that they have either created or acquired. For example, a presentation is a thing that you create. So, for my business, the vehicle is a presentation. It is the thing that my clients use to get the result that they want.

Depending on the context of the business, you can have many different thing vehicles.

For example, let's say someone was a marketing expert and they helped people get clients through using Facebook groups. The thing vehicle for them would be a Facebook group. If you were a strategic consultant that helped organizations with their people planning, then the thing vehicle could be a strategic people plan. If you were a coach that helped organizations build a coaching culture within their leadership, then the thing vehicle could be a coaching culture.

As you can see, a thing vehicle is something that is external from the person—it's almost like a project or somewhat of an outcome. Think about what you do and consider whether there is a thing that people use to get the outcome they want.

The Skill Vehicle

The next type of vehicle is what I refer to as a skill vehicle. This is the type of vehicle whereby someone develops a skill set to produce the result they want. The good news is that you can have both a thing vehicle and a skill vehicle. For me, my thing vehicle is a presentation, but my skill vehicle is selling from the stage. There are obviously many ways I could say this—it could also be persuasive speaking or speaking in a way that sells. But essentially, I'm describing a skill that someone develops to get a result they want.

The most important thing here is that it's identified as a skill that someone develops. It's something that becomes part of them as opposed to an external mechanism that they use. As an example, let's say you are a parenting coach; then your skill vehicle is parenting skills. If you are a leadership coach, then the skill that you help develop within leaders is leadership coaching skills. If you are an innovation consultant, then the skill you help develop is innovative thinking. If you are a life coach, then the skill you might help people develop is an empowered mindset.

As you can see, all of these are descriptors of skill sets that your clients can develop to get the result that they want. A skill vehicle is fantastic for many service-based entrepreneurs and consultants who are helping their clients develop a skill set.

The Identity Vehicle

The third type of vehicle is what I refer to as an identity vehicle. An identity is essentially the name you give to a made-up character. It sounds kind of odd even writing this that you literally make up an identity that your prospects inevitably strive to become. But it's one of the most powerful marketing tools you can create. Once you understand what an identity vehicle is, you'll most probably look around in the marketplace and notice them everywhere. Essentially, it is a description of a type of person you declare as being successful.

The identity vehicle that I use is an irresistible speaker. The secret is that after you state the identity, you can describe the characteristics of this person. For example, for me, an irresistible speaker is someone who communicates in a way that naturally attracts clients. They aren't chasing clients— their clients are chasing them. That's the power of becoming an irresistible speaker.

Now I want you to know that I just made up that character name. All I did was put a descriptive word in front of a category. I called the successful person an irresistible speaker, and in doing that, it creates a magnetism toward wanting to become that. The good part about this vehicle is that you can make it up. And the simplest way of doing that is just having a description word in front of a category word.

One of my good friends, James Wedmore, who is an established expert in the online space, has an identity that he calls a Digital CEO. James has essentially built a multimillion-dollar business around two words. Obviously, there is more to it than that, but the Digital CEO identity is at the heart of his message. If you end up experiencing some of his marketing, you'll notice that he uses the phrase Digital CEO all the time. In fact, it forms the foundation for the direction of his marketing campaigns.

James's core premise is that he helps you become a Digital CEO. When you join one of his courses or programs, he even sometimes sends out a desk placard that says "Digital CEO." He's a brilliant marketer, but what he's done here is create an identity that people who want to build online businesses desire to become.

One of my clients, Larry, uses what he calls a Freedom Physician. He helps doctors free themselves up from being a slave to their work by adding additional cash flow to their income through multifamily housing. This identity of being a Freedom Physician is one of the cool focuses of his messaging in the marketplace. It forms a powerful frame for prospects to want to achieve.

These are all different examples of identity vehicles that people are using in the marketplace effectively to create a magnetic pull from a prospect to a client. Go ahead and create your own identity vehicle; it is fun and highly effective.

The Unique Vehicle

The last type of vehicle that I've noticed people utilize is a unique vehicle. This is essentially where you create your own unique name or methodology for what you do. For example, I have a unique vehicle that I call the Conversion Story Formula. Originally I was going to call it simply a signature story, and then after a conversation with my good friend, Brendan Lucero, we landed on the concept of a conversion story.

In my industry, I hadn't heard anyone talking about a conversion story, so when I came to market with this concept, it immediately piqued people's interest. I had high-level masterminds asking me to come and speak to their entire client group about this one concept. I'll talk about your conversion story in Chapter 9, but I want you to know that I simply made this term up. But this term makes me a lot of money as it positions my expertise in a unique frame.

Another unique vehicle that I've come up with is Infusion Selling®. Infusion Selling is a concept that I coined whereby you can provide value in your presentation and also sell at the same time. I'm sure there are other people in the marketplace who are teaching a similar concept, but no one has called it Infusion Selling. When you give a name to something that you do, it instantly becomes more valuable in the marketplace. So, essentially, you want to consider what you help people do and come up with a unique name or description for that methodology.

The second part of a core premise is the result; let's discuss how you can describe the result.

Results

Prospects come to work with you because they want a result. I think most entrepreneurs lose sight of that—we get really caught up with how cool our ideas are and all the steps in our processes, but really, all people want is a result.

It's important to describe this result in a clear manner. For me, I've described it in a really simple way, which is creating a business breakthrough. I could also describe the result that I help people with as growing their business, increasing their client base, or getting a flood of clients. These are all different ways of describing the outcome that I help people achieve.

Think about your audience and what they want. Usually, you can describe this in both emotional and result-based terms. For example, maybe they want more meaning in their life or better connection with their family. You don't have to get too fancy with this, but it is important to clearly articulate what your prospects want.

Pulling It All Together

Now that you understand that to create a core premise, you need a vehicle and a result, what you're going to do is choose one of the four vehicle types and combine it with an outcome that your clients want. Here are some examples of core premises using each vehicle type and a result:

- A thing-based core premise could be: "Engaged Facebook groups are the most effective way to build a community and attract your ideal clients into your business." The vehicle here is Facebook groups, and the result is building a community and attracting ideal clients.
- A skill-based core premise could be: "Developing leadership coaching skills is the most effective way to get the most from your employees and team." The vehicle here is developing leadership skills, and the result is getting the most from their employees and team.

- An identity-based core premise could be: "Becoming an irresistible speaker is the most effective way to attract clients and build the business of your dreams." The vehicle here is becoming an irresistible entrepreneur, and the result is attracting clients and building the business of your dreams.

- A unique vehicle-based core premise could be (this is one of mine): "Creating your conversion story is the most effective way to instantly connect with your audience and draw them toward your offers." The vehicle here is a conversion story, and the result is connecting with your audience and drawing them toward your offer.

These are all different examples of the same core premise structure using thing, skill, identity, or unique vehicle types. As you can see, there is no one perfect way of writing a core premise—the most important thing is that you have one. Consider the way that you help clients get a result and put it into a single sentence.

I've helped thousands of clients do this, and the value it adds to their business is immense. Creating your core premise is the fastest and most effective way to have clarity in your message so you can attract your dream clients. See what I did just there? I created a core premise for a core premise.

Now that you understand the core premise, we can move on to building an irresistible offer that your clients will desperately desire.

Chapter 5

The Irresistible Offer

I'd been working on my offer for six months. Every moment I had between clients, I would write the curriculum for my online course offer and envision how powerful it would be putting it out there in the world. The day came when I decided it was time to officially create and launch it! I booked a videographer and a studio to create the program. I spent three days in the studio delivering the best I could. My videographer edited everything, and we built out the online program.

As I approached the first promotion, I was nervous and anxious, but I was also really excited. I started promoting it on social media and talking about it everywhere. The promotion was designed as a three-part video series that led into an open-cart period where people could enroll. The surprising thing was that I ended up getting more than 600 people to sign up for the promotion.

I was so excited about how many people were going to potentially join the course and how much money I could make. I remember saying to myself, "I feel like I'm going to make more than $10,000 . . . no, hang on, I think I could make more than $100,000 based on how many people have signed up for this promotion!"

The day came when we opened the cart to the group of prospects, and no one joined. Absolute crickets. It came to day two, and I thought, "I'm sure people are going to join today," but no one joined. I started to think there might be something wrong with the checkout, so I decided to buy the course myself, and sure enough, the checkout worked perfectly. The problem was that no one was going through the checkout. The next few days, I was bitterly disappointed. No one bought my course, and I felt completely deflated. On the last day of the promotional period, in the final four hours, someone joined at the lowest monthly installment plan. As much as I was grateful for that one person joining, I was devastated because I had just lost more than $5,000 in the creation and promotion of the course.

Change Your Offer, Not Your Program

After no one actually took my course, I started to question whether it was something that people even wanted. It was a topic that I had been delivering with my one-on-one coaching clients, but I'd never packaged it up into an online offering. After many discussions with my wife and questioning the meaning of life, I eventually came to the realization that the content in my course was actually really good. The feedback I'd gotten from clients who had been through my processes was very positive. So I knew my course materials were great, or at least good enough—the problem was that I didn't know how to articulate the value of the course materials to interested prospects.

Over the next few months, I became obsessed with how to create content that generated desire for the program I was selling. I went to my audience of 600 people who went through the promotion and didn't buy and asked them what stopped them from purchasing my program. The information they gave me was incredible. They talked about elements that were missing in the program that, if included, would have made them join. They told me that the program looked really good, but they weren't sure if it was right for them. They told me that the program didn't seem to have a clear outcome. They shared that they wanted more help and coaching in the program.

All of this material formed the basis for re-creating my offer and relaunching it to the world. Within about 90 days, I had rebuilt a 60-minute presentation and added some special bonuses to the exact program that didn't sell previously. After this first presentation, I remember getting three enrollments and making more than $3,000 dollars. This was really exciting because even though not as many people signed up for the presentation, a greater percentage of people bought it. Then I started refining this presentation every single month, getting more feedback on the offer, making it actually irresistible. Over the next three years of promoting this online course that no one initially seemed interested in, I ended up enrolling 2,427 people.

Going through this experience, I realized that you can have amazing course materials and content, but if you don't know how to articulate the value of that content, then people might not buy it. I learned that your program is different from your offer. I want you to think about your offer as being the skin that surrounds the program. The good news is that you probably have a really good program—you just haven't made it into an irresistible offer.

Even better than this is that you don't necessarily have to change or re-create your program to change your offer. Your offer is essentially the way you articulate the value of the program. This means you can change your offer without needing to completely change your program.

Start with Your Offer

I always recommend people start with their offer. The reason why you should start with the offer is, as Stephen Covey, author of *The 7 Habits of Highly Effective People*, says, to "begin with the end in mind." Your end goal is that people would join your programs, so you need to build back from that endpoint to ensure everything is going in the right direction.

Many people make the mistake of creating a sales presentation without really considering the offer itself. Sure, they might have a vague idea of what their offer is, but they haven't developed a clear structure and outcome for their program. When this occurs, you'll end up with a mismatch between the content you deliver in your signature talk and the offer itself. The more synergy you can create between the signature presentation and the irresistible offer, the more clients you'll get.

As we explore creating an irresistible offer, there are some mindset and strategic nuances you must be aware of to make this work. Let's explore them now.

A Sacred Place of Transformation

Most people have the wrong perspective of what an offer is. Many think the goal of an offer is to get as many people into their program as possible to maximize profits. This is a mistake. This mindset will cost you both energetically, because the wrong people will join your program, and monetarily, because your offer will come from a place of desperation rather than protection.

My definition of an offer is that it's a "sacred place of transformation." Think about any sacred place—what is usually required of you? You might have to take off your shoes, lower your voice, or take a different stance. When someone enters the space of your offer, they should feel like they're entering a sacred place. It's a special environment where they can experience a greater level of transformation than they would have outside.

There are three currencies that protect an offer: money, energy, and time. In Figure 5.1 you can see that inside the small circle is your offer, and the outside circle represents the external environment. The circle surrounding the offer acts as a wall of commitment. The greater the requirements, usually the more sacred the space is inside that offer. For instance, joining a $27 program is very different from joining a $27,000 program.

You can use energy to protect your offer by interviewing people to determine if they're an energetic fit for the group. We all know how disruptive it can be when you get the wrong

Figure 5.1 Protecting your offer

person in your offer. I'm not saying you need to be so protective that you allow only a few people to join your program, but the higher the requirements for entering the offer, usually the more sacred the offer will feel.

Many people feel bad about asking for money during their pitch, but I want you to start viewing money as a currency of commitment. Your offer comprises three currencies of commitment: money, time, and energy. Their combination increases commitment. When you shift your mindset to see money as a currency of commitment, you'll realize that the client paying money actually increases their commitment level. Online expert and coach James Wedmore has always said to me, "The transformation starts with the transaction." When someone pays money, they pay attention. Their transformative process begins as they invest in themself in your program.

Think about how many times you've had access to a free course or community and done nothing with it. If you had paid $1,000 or $10,000 for access, you would have been much more involved. Even if everything else stayed the same, your commitment and engagement would naturally increase simply because you paid money. This means you can stop feeling bad about asking for money and realize you're just asking people to commit more deeply to the outcomes they already desire.

I remember the first time I joined a high-level mastermind program—I had just completed the initial interview with the leader of the mastermind. He'd asked me a few questions about my business philosophy and how I might be able to add value to the group itself. We finished the conversation, and he didn't say whether I was accepted into the program. I didn't know the actual price to join the mastermind, but I thought it might be expensive. I'll never forget getting an email two days later saying that based on the interview they would like to invite me to join and that the cost is $25,000.

When I learned the price, I told my wife it was way too much money. But my wife is incredible; she challenged me and said she really felt it was the next step for our business. Despite the fear, I decided to say yes to this program. To say that it changed my life is an understatement.

It created a space for me to make some of the best friends I've ever made in my entire life, whom I still catch up with regularly. It showed me a vision of a bigger future and gave me the strategies and confidence to build a seven-figure coaching business. It truly was a sacred place of transformation. Without entering that environment, I would not have achieved what I have achieved, and that is what I want for your offers as well.

This level of protection makes your offer more attractive. It's remarkable what happens when you protect your offer instead of trying to get anyone with a heartbeat to join. Obviously, lower-ticket offers have lower barriers to entry. We have offers under $100 that thousands join yearly, and I don't individually screen them. However, as you move up the levels and get more access to me and my team, we become more protective. It's one reason we get such great feedback because our community is amazing and people feel the sacredness of the environment.

Your prospects desperately want to see change in their lives—whether improving their health, finding their perfect partner, or building a business that provides financial and lifestyle freedom. This transformation should happen faster, more easily, and more efficiently when they join your program. When the prospect's desired outcome aligns with the offer's outcome and your offer has integrity in its delivery, it creates true transformation.

They Buy Your Certainty

People buy a feeling. To be more specific, the feeling that people buy is certainty. Your prospect is coming to you with a high degree of uncertainty. They have a desire for what they want to achieve in their life, but they feel uncertain, unclear, and overwhelmed about how to achieve it. Part of making an offer irresistible starts with the certainty you communicate your offer with.

Your prospects already have enough uncertainty in their life—what they're looking for is leadership. Certainty, or another flavor of that being confidence, is one of the most attractive and powerful reasons why they would say yes to your offer.

The problem is that many people struggle to develop high levels of certainty. Maybe you are delivering a webinar and it comes to the pitch at the end, and you start feeling really unsure of yourself. Or you're sitting in front of a prospect on a sales call, and when it gets to the point where you have to deliver the offer, you start freaking out.

So you are probably asking, "How do I increase my certainty to make offers?" There are three levels of certainty that you can develop. By going through these three levels, you will gain greater confidence and therefore start selling more effortlessly to your prospects.

The first level of certainty comes from Personal Certainty. Many of the people I work with have usually been through some level of transformative experience with the process they are helping other people with. For example, many health coaches have been on a big health journey themselves, or if you're a life coach, you've experienced some breakthroughs personally from being coached. If you're a business coach, you've probably either built a business or been mentored by a business leader and learned a business building methodology that has had a big impact on your life. This first level of certainty is essentially about you feeling like what you want to help people with has already had an impact on you personally.

The second level of certainty comes when you have Process Certainty. Process Certainty is when you've spent the time to map out the specific process of transformation that you are taking your clients through. One of the reasons why people don't buy your program is because it's confusing. I always like to have anywhere between three to five main pillars of a program. Any less than that can feel underwhelming, and any more than that can feel overwhelming. Spending the time to map out, in a logical manner, the transformation or process that your clients will experience when they enter your offer gives you certainty in presenting and selling, and it gives the prospect clarity as to how they will achieve their transformation.

The final level of certainty comes when you have Proof Certainty. This is essentially you getting enough social proof that what you teach can be transferred to other people. I regularly read through the testimonials and transformations that my clients send me. As much as it makes me feel great that I've helped other people, it also gives me more confidence in my offer. I encourage you to be very purposeful when it comes to gathering testimonials.

But you might still be thinking, "I don't have much external proof or testimonials to give me the confidence I need to sell my products." One of the best things you can do to increase your confidence is to give away your services for free at the start of your business journey. When I first started my life coaching practice, I gave away six coaching sessions to 10 individuals in the marketplace. I did 60 hours of free coaching before I ever made any paid coaching offers. I can't express how much my confidence grew through this process. I got to see firsthand that I had the skills to create transformation in people's lives, it gave me clarity in the process of how I facilitated that transformation, and then they gave me raving reviews and video testimonials about the impact it had on their lives.

It was from that moment that my confidence dramatically rose, and the next time I was sitting in front of a prospect and saying that my services were several thousand dollars, I could say it with a sense of certainty. In fact, the first time I shared with a prospect that my coaching services were a couple of thousand dollars, he said, "Sounds great, when do we start?" I was taken by surprise—it was almost like I didn't actually believe it. I remember thinking in my mind, "But wait, are you sure?" He was sure, and the coaching we did together had a deep impact on his life, his marriage, and his business. We got to have a sacred experience together that I'm forever grateful for.

The Elements of an Offer

Now, let's break down the elements of an offer itself. There are nine essential elements you must understand to build out your offer:

1. Name

2. Promise

3. Modules

4. Bonuses

5. Guarantee

6. Social proof

7. Price

8. Scarcity

9. Aesthetics

Name

The first key element is the name of the offer. Creating a name that is both distinctive and compelling is crucial to making your offer irresistible.

A great way to think about your offer name is to consider three things: what your program does, who it's for, and the type of delivery involved. Let's start with what your program does. For example, if you're creating a health coaching program, consider what it accomplishes. Let's use the example of a health coach; your program creates energy, vitality, weight loss, and confidence—these are just a few examples. Next, consider who it's for—it could be for executive men or executive women. Finally, think about how the program is actually delivered. It could be an online course, coaching program, mastermind, or individual private coaching. The delivery method will impact the name of the program itself.

Let's take these three considerations and create a name. We could create a program called "Executive Edge Fitness Coaching" or "Women With Energy Online Course." You could also simply state what it is, such as "Master Your Fitness Coaching Program." For me, after playing around with hundreds of different variations, I decided to call our main signature program exactly what it teaches: "Sell From Stage Academy®." It helps people sell their courses and coaching programs from a stage, whether virtual or in person. While I experimented with different titles, I do love calling programs exactly what they do.

Sometimes using the literal name of what you're teaching people to do works best as the program name.

When it comes down to it, while the name is important, it's sometimes not as crucial as we think. Your audience will create an association with the name of your program over time. There are some incredibly successful courses and masterminds out there that are simply named with one or two words like "Ignite," "Expansion," "Power Player," or "Next Level." Ultimately, it's about finding a name that you and your audience resonate with and that explains, on some level, what your program does.

Promise

The second element of creating an offer is clarifying your outcome. Your outcome is the end destination that you're offering to your audience. As an important side note, your audience doesn't want your program—they want the outcome that your program gives them. Knowing how to clearly articulate your outcome is crucial because it should be incredibly enticing and desirable for your audience when they hear it.

The outcome of my program is "The step-by-step system for coaches and experts to build a high-converting presentation that gets them clients every single time they speak." Let's break down this structure. I started the outcome with phrasing like "the step-by-step program," "the comprehensive program," or "the ultimate guide to." Then you describe either who it's for or what outcome it creates. For example, with the health example, I could say that the Executive Edge Fitness Coaching outcome is "The step-by-step coaching program for executives who want to lose weight, regain their energy, and look better than they ever have in their life."

Modules

The next element is modules. You need to break down the big stepping-stones that people need to move through to get the results you can help them achieve. Using the health coaching example, you could say that the five big stepping-stones are building a health mindset, understanding your body, building a custom eating plan, creating a fitness routine, and getting accountability in place. As long as there is a logical pathway through the modules or process you're proposing, you're doing the right thing at this stage.

Bonuses

Next, let's discuss bonuses. Many people don't understand the purpose of bonuses, and you'll often see offers in the market-place with random, overwhelming bonuses. When done right, bonuses are one of the most important parts of the offer. The purpose of a bonus is to either heighten desire for someone to want to do your program or handle a specific objection that would stop them from moving forward.

For example, in the health coaching scenario, you could create a desire-based bonus, such as personalized vitamins delivered to their door based on testing done in phase one. Getting a physical product delivered monthly that's easy to take and provides immediate benefits is an incredibly desirable bonus. Another desirable bonus could be an invitation to an in-person or virtual workshop where they can learn more about their fitness, lifestyle, and energy improvement.

The second type of bonus is an objection-based bonus, which addresses specific resistances your prospects might have. For example, one objection in a health coaching program might be that clients don't know how to food shop efficiently and effectively. You could create a bonus where you provide them with a consultation to build out their regular shopping list online, making it as simple as ordering what you recommend each month. Another common resistance is feeling uncomfortable at the gym, so you could create a bonus showing them how to work out at home, which also addresses the resistance of requiring extra time away from home.

The bonuses in my signature program Sell From Stage Academy® were created over a 12-month period based on feedback from people who didn't buy our program. What most people don't understand is how valuable it is to ask people why they chose not to buy.

One of the common reasons people gave for not buying our program was that they didn't know how to get people registered for the virtual presentations that I was promising to help them with. In response, I created an objection-based bonus called "Your First 100 Virtual Attendees." This bonus was designed to show them how to organically get 100 or more people registered for a virtual presentation where they could make their offer. As a result, this bonus increased our conversion rates and effectively handled the objection of not having enough leads.

Guarantee

Think of your guarantee like a life raft if things don't go as planned. Your guarantee gives your prospect a sense of safety and certainty when they are taking the risk of purchasing your offer. Depending on the industry you're in, you need to be cautious of the types of guarantees you give. But as a generalization, there are three main types of guarantees you can offer:

- **A no-questions-asked money-back guarantee based on a time frame:** This is the ultimate guarantee, essentially offering your customer a chance to get their money back within a set time period (let's say 30 days) for absolutely any reason they want. Their dog could be feeling sick on Thursday, and that's the reason they ask for a refund, and you have to give it. This provides a lot of safety for the client and will usually dramatically increase the number of purchases because customers feel very comfortable about getting their money back if the program isn't the right fit for them. This will obviously increase the number of refunds you'll be giving, so you need to weigh up the advantages and disadvantages of this based on your particular offer.

- **A working or conditional guarantee:** This is where you require the customer to do a specific set of actions or tasks to qualify for the guarantee. This could be watching a set number of modules, taking specific actions, or turning up to live sessions. I like this kind of guarantee because it encourages people to purchase the program only if they are committed to taking some action. Just make sure it's really clear what needs to be completed in order for them to qualify for any type of refund. The more actions you're requiring them to take, the less safety the customer will feel, so you need to find the right balance of requirements so they at least feel like the conditional guarantee is achievable.

- **Having no guarantee:** This is where you state that there are no refunds. There's also something powerful about saying to your audience that their purchase is final. When you decide to have no guarantee, it essentially says to the customer that you only want them to join if they are fully committed to the outcome. This will generally attract more committed buyers, but it will reduce the number of clients you convert.

Due to laws, regulations, and culture, some of these rules and conditions do change depending on the countries you're in, so please speak with a professional when you are finalizing your guarantee. I personally love a conditional guarantee as it puts some onus on the customer to take action but also gives them a sense of safety that if the program or product is really not right for them, they have a way out.

Social Proof

When you're walking through a mall and you see a group of people surrounding a busker, there is something within you that wants to head over and take a look at why there are so many people watching. This is the intuitive power of social proof. When you see other people having a great experience, you automatically feel drawn toward considering that experience for yourself.

I was first introduced to the power of social proof by Robert Cialdini in his famous book *Influence*. He talks about how social proof is one of the most powerful persuasion strategies for selling products, programs, and ideas. Essentially, what we're talking about here is gathering enough testimonials, clients' reviews, and case studies to show your prospects that there are people just like them who have had success with your program.

I feel like most people don't prioritize gathering social proof enough. Personally, I screenshot any type of positive feedback we get from our programs. I'll regularly ask for video and written testimonials when I see someone post in our online groups about a transformation or win they've just experienced. And with permission, I will share their experience in my presentations and sales pages.

Let's get a little more advanced when it comes to social proof. There are three ways that you can use it:

- **Result-based testimonials:** Gathering testimonials from clients who talk about the general experience and results with your programs and products. These are great because they show what's possible and showcase the integrity of what you do. This is the foundational level of social proof where a customer has experienced a problem, used one of your strategies, and now is experiencing a better life because of it.

- **Objection-based testimonials:** This is where you gather testimonials that address a very specific objection. Before asking your client to provide you a testimonial, ask them what objections or resistances they experienced before joining your program. They might say that before joining, they felt like they weren't ready or they didn't have enough money at the time. You can ask them to share this objection as part of their testimonial and how they overcame this resistance to eventually enroll in your program and then the results they got from working with you. Obviously, you can't tell your customer what to say, but if that was their experience, it's very powerful to have them articulate in their own language what their objections were and how they personally overcame them.

- **Celebrity social proof:** This is where you get endorsements or testimonials from people who have social clout or celebrity in your industry. Usually, you won't have access to these types of testimonials right away, but as you get good at your craft, you'll come across opportunities where getting an endorsement from someone who has credibility in your industry is extremely powerful.

When you start out with a brand-new program or product, you probably won't have much social proof. This is why you should launch your initial product as a pilot version, sometimes referred to as a beta program. The first time I launched Sell From Stage Academy®, I didn't have any testimonials from my ideal client, so the initial program was launched at a heavily discounted rate. After the pilot program was completed, I had more than 30+ testimonials from clients who had been through this initial program and already achieved results. This formed the foundation for relaunching the program at its full price.

The most important thing to do is act quickly on client wins when you see them. So often a client will send you an email telling you about an amazing result they just achieved. You'll read the email and think "wow, that's so cool," feel really good for a couple of minutes, and then move on to the next email. This is your opportunity to gather incredible social proof. Write back to them and ask if they would be willing to shoot a short video sharing their experience of the challenge they once had and the results they've now achieved through your program. Once you receive this, with their permission, you'll be able to turn it into written formats, case studies, and many other ways.

Price

Pricing your program is one of the most important decisions you'll ever make. It's really interesting how the market will respond to price. I've had times when I've doubled the price of a program, and it actually increased the number of people purchasing it. The price of your program sends a message to your audience as to the value of what you deliver.

In pricing your program, you do need to consider who your audience is and the service you offer. I have friends who run $37-a-month online fitness memberships and make more than $10 million a year. Obviously, you have to have a lot of customers to do that, but just because you have a lower price doesn't mean you can't make a lot of money. You need to understand who your customers are and price according to them and the industry.

When building out your programs and products, you'll tend to have three levels:

- A low-ticket or introductory offer
- A mid-ticket or signature offer
- A high-ticket or premium offer

I always recommend our Sell From Stage students to start with their mid-ticket signature offer. The reason is that you don't need huge credibility to launch a program at this level, and if you sell a few of these products, you'll start making enough money to go full-time in your business quickly. Depending on the industry you're in, a signature offer will vary, but as a generalization, it's usually anywhere between $500 to $3,000. This is a great price point to offer on the back of a presentation, and it doesn't require extensive sales calls or extended decision time for people.

Once you get your signature offer selling, you can then choose to either add a lower-ticket or a high-ticket offer in the mix. I've noticed that most people add extra offers too quickly. I think you are better off refining your presentation and offer until it gets to a point where it is very reliable and predictable. If you add a premium or low-ticket offer in the mix too quickly, you will be distracted and it will take away from the progress you're making with your mid-ticket offer.

Once you get your mid-ticket offer selling well, adding a low-ticket offer can be amazing for generating quality leads into your communty. For example, we have a mini course called Conversion Story Formula, and it's the cost of a few California-priced tacos. It gives people a chance to experience the quality of my content, which results in many of those people joining our more premium offerings.

You can also add a high-ticket or premium offer to the mix. This should be three to five times the price of your mid-ticket offer. I've found there are always at least 10% of your customers who are willing to pay a lot more than they currently are paying. Adding a premium experience to your offer suite is a great way to add profitability to your business. For example, if you have a mid-tier program at $1,000, then adding a premium experience at around $3,000 to $5,000 will make the mid-tier program feel inexpensive, and it will also attract premium customers who are willing to invest more for greater access to you or your team.

The exact price that you choose will be based on your own personal preferences and the feedback of your audience. I personally love to price things finishing with a seven or nine. There's a lot of data to suggest that numbers finishing with seven or nine tend to convert higher. Generally, I wouldn't finish with a whole number—for example, if you are going to sell a program for $500, I recommend selling it for $497 or $499. Pricing your product just below the whole number psychologically reduces the price and makes the decision easier for the prospect. So if you have a program that's a thousand dollars, make it $997 or $999.

Have fun and experiment with your pricing and make sure to deliver an experience that the customer genuinely feels was worth 10 times the investment they made.

Scarcity

One of the most uncomfortable things humans can do is make a decision. For most people, making a decision feels scary. There is an increase in responsibility when we make a decision to move forward or go in a different direction. For most of your prospects, they would prefer not to make a decision—this is why scarcity is so important. Scarcity, in my mind, supercharges your prospects' ability to make a decision because essentially it says to them that if they don't decide, the decision will be made for them.

Sometimes, I'll have a conversation with a student where they'll say they aren't getting the sales they were hoping for from their presentation. After a short discussion, I realized that they were missing this one element: scarcity. For most of them, it's as simple as adding a deadline or cut-off date for when your prospects must enroll—this is referred to as time-based scarcity.

As soon as they added scarcity into their offer, sales increased instantly. For example, if you hosted an online presentation, giving people five days to make a decision will usually increase conversion rates compared to saying that it's open for enrollment at any time.

There are many other types of scarcity that you can utilize to increase the number of people joining your programs. A couple of common ones include:

- **Availability scarcity:** This is where you have a limited number of spots or you have only limited stock available. You will see this on Amazon or different websites, where when you are looking at an item it will say there are only three left. When you see there are only three left, you'll find yourself quickly saying to your partner, "We probably should buy this right now so that we don't miss out." That's the power of scarcity influencing your decision.

- **Fast action scarcity:** This is whereby you reward people who decide to join in a shorter period of time. For example, maybe you have open enrollment for five days, but for the first 24 hours, you offer a special bonus. This is fantastic for rewarding those people who are ready to make a decision right now and are committed to working with you.

- **Deadline scarcity:** This is where you simply provide a deadline for when everyone must decide to either join or not join. Having a clear cut-off time and date works wonders for getting prospects who are on the fence to make a decision.

Make sure to have some type of scarcity in your offer because it will supercharge your prospects' ability to make a decision.

Aesthetics

The final piece of your offer is ensuring that it looks visually appealing. I'm not a designer myself, but I appreciate the impact of aesthetics on a sales page or brochure. The visual aspect of your offer includes selecting colors and fonts that reflect your brand and resonate with your audience. It also involves choosing high-quality images that enhance the presentation. A great way to make your offer more compelling is to showcase the workbooks, templates, and tools your prospects will receive—demonstrating how these resources will help them achieve results faster.

These are the nine core elements of building an irresistible offer. Most people believe their offer is simply their program or product, but as you can see, your offer is much more than that. It is the articulation of the results and benefits your clients will gain and it includes the persuasive elements such as social proof, guarantees, scarcity, pricing, and aesthetics. Once you create an offer that truly resonates with your audience, you'll have a strong foundation upon which to build a profitable and successful business.

Case Study Breakout: How Wendy Snyder Increased 5X Her Sales Results

Wendy is a parenting coach with a thriving online membership called Fresh Start Family. However, she wanted to launch a higher-ticket certification program to help other parents become parenting coaches themselves. The initial launch of her certification didn't get the results she was after. She got a few enrollments, but most of the feedback she received was that the program was not necessarily for them or it was out of their price range.

There were two things she needed to change to see a different result. First, she needed to upgrade the offer. She didn't necessarily change the program, but she changed how she presented the offer, making it more aligned with the outcomes people were looking for based on the feedback she got from her first round. Second, she changed her signature talk, which she was going to use as an online webinar to launch the program in the second round.

She delivered this new signature talk based on the Sell From Stage structure, and she ended up enrolling five times the number of students compared to her previous round. She was over the moon because not only did the business grow significantly, but she was able to impact more parents' lives with the powerful parenting tools she teaches. She now has an offer and signature talk that she can use over and over again to create the impact she's always desired.

Chapter 6

Identify Your Audience

Most people don't understand how important their chosen audience is. The truth is, you can have the most amazing offer and an incredible signature talk, but if your audience isn't the right fit, you won't make much money.

You need to remember that the audience you choose is going to impact your life significantly. You'll be spending a lot of time with these people, thinking about their problems, the desires they feel, and the results they want. Choosing your ideal audience is crucial in this process.

Many entrepreneurs I speak with struggle because they haven't identified their ideal audience. Most people are extremely broad—I know I was when I first started my business. The problem with being broad is that it's difficult to speak to your audience directly. You'll tend to use vague language that doesn't really connect with anyone. The old saying "If you speak to everyone, you speak to no one" is especially true when it comes to marketing.

Some of my most successful students started with a broad audience and then narrowed down to a really specific audience, which has created much more success in their business. The term that many people use in the industry is their "niche." For me, your niche comprises two things: the audience you're focused on and the message you're delivering to that audience.

Throughout the book we look at delivering your message, so in this chapter, I want to focus on the audience itself.

In identifying your audience, I believe there are two levels of understanding them: demographics and psychographics. Demographics consist of age, location, gender, religion, income, interests, and so on. I'm most interested in psychographics because these are the motivating factors for why people will buy your program. But let's start first with demographics.

Understand the Demographics

Demographics are the classical criteria that many marketers have used to clarify who exactly they are focused on. This includes:

- Age
- Gender
- Interests
- Income
- Country
- Language
- Education
- Ethnicity
- Family
- Career
- Size

When you're identifying your audience, you don't have to be hyperspecific on every single one of these criteria, but it's valuable to spend time identifying the more focused characteristics within this list that would impact you and your results.

For example, let's say you work with women aged 45–55 with interests in homesteading, gardening, and horticulture, based in the United States and Canada, speaking English, with a college-level education and a family with two or more kids. Just identifying these specifics will help you know where to find them and how to serve them.

One of the reasons why demographics are so important is that they help you find these people. The problem with having a really broad audience demographic is that they're difficult to find. If you know your audience is interested in homesteading, then you can go on social media platforms and join home-steading groups. It's important to understand demographics because they will shape the examples, stories, metaphors, and messages you use. However, the most powerful thing you can understand is what's going on inside their hearts and minds—this is essentially the psychographics.

Unpack Their Psychographics

I was standing in the playground while my daughter, Georgia, who was about four years old at the time, was playing with her friends. I'll be honest with you, I was looking at my phone more than I was watching her. I started to hear her shout out to me. At the top of her little voice she's screaming, "Dad, come over here! Dad, come here now!" I looked up for a minute, waved, and then looked back down at my phone.

In my mind I told myself she is fine, I've got important mes-sages to get back to. Little did I know that while I was focused on my phone again, Georgia had walked over to me and was standing right next to me and started tapping my leg. I looked down to see her two blonde pigtails and her blue eyes looking up at me with her hand over her mouth like as if she wanted to tell something to me.

I bent down and she cupped my ear with her hand and she whispered, "Dad, I'm really scared to go across the playground, and I have my other friends over there. Could you hold my hand and take me across?" It was at that moment that the proverbial dagger went into my heart and I realized that I had a Dad fail. I grabbed her hand in mine, and we walked across the playground so that she could play with her friends.

As I reflected on that moment, I realized that when she was shouting at me across the playground, I wasn't responding. I was distracted by my own world. But it wasn't until she came close and whispered into my ear the words that would instantly move my heart as a dad that I took action.

This is the power of whispering the right words into your audience's ear. It's not about shouting or getting aggressive; it's about deeply understanding what your audience is going through and whispering the right words into their hearts and minds so that they instantly feel like you get them. Let's now learn how to whisper.

To move your audience, you must understand the main drivers that shape human behavior. The first is wanting to avoid things that are painful, and the second is wanting to move toward things that are pleasurable. Moving away from pain and toward pleasure are the two psychological levers you must be familiar with to be a persuasive communicator. In fact, at the opening of your presentation, you'll spend a lot of time digging deep into the pain and pleasure that this audience experiences.

Pain Drivers

Let's consider pain drivers. For example, if I were doing a presentation for coaches and course creators who want to sell their online courses using a presentation, I could dive into some of their pains by saying this to them:

> "As a coach or course creator, one of the most difficult parts of selling your online course through a presentation is knowing what to put in and what to leave out. It can be incredibly confusing working out how much information you should share while trying not to overwhelm your audience. The second challenge is that after you design your presentation, there's an overwhelming fear that the audience may not resonate with or might even dislike your presentation. You'll also fear what happens if you deliver your presentation and people like it, but no one buys your program. This can feel incredibly disheartening as a business owner. You'll end up lying awake at night worrying about whether you're going to make enough money to build your business and how you can explain that worry to your partner or even your kids."

I just went into the pain that many in my audience experience when preparing or delivering a presentation to sell their programs. Ideally, at some point, while reading that paragraph, you could feel the internal discomfort rising in you and the concerns awakening inside. That's how your audience should feel when you're digging deep into their pains and challenges.

You want them to feel the pain and also answer the first important question: "Does this presenter really understand my concerns?"

Based on thousands of presentations I've delivered and working with many clients, I've noticed it's usually easier to start with the pain people are experiencing rather than their desires and pleasures. When doing a presentation, if you start talking about goals and desires before addressing pain and concerns, you tend to encounter internal resistance. So, you always want to dig deep into people's pain before addressing their pleasure.

Here is another example using a different target audience. Let's say you want to speak to women interested in homesteading for their family. You could say something like:

> "As a mom who is committed to creating healthy, vibrant kids, it is a real challenge to afford to pay for organic food all the time. You find yourself in the supermarket struggling to justify the cost of organically grown vegetables and fruits. Maybe you've tried to grow them yourself at home, but you've struggled to produce enough food to make one meal, let alone feed a family. It can feel really disheartening knowing that you have to settle on the lower quality produce for your family, especially because they are the people you care about the most."

If you are a mom who wants to create a homesteading lifestyle for your family, when you read that, there was probably something that emotively triggered in you. This is the power of whispering the words that your audience wants to hear.

Pleasure Drivers

Now, let's transition and talk about pleasure. Every human being has a desire to move toward things they want. Continuing with the same example of my audience, here is how I might address some things they desire:

> "As an entrepreneur, one of your desires is to present your message in a clear and confident way. You want to feel like the message you're sharing is really impacting people's lives and motivating them to see a change. You also have a desire to grow your business and make money. You want to show not only your family and friends, but ultimately yourself, that you are able to create an impact and generate an income that represents a life of courage."

Ideally, when you read that last paragraph, something within you resonated with those ideas. As you read it, you may have been thinking that you too, would love to create a clear message, connect with your audience, make amazing money, and leave a legacy for you and your family that may not have existed in previous generations.

Once again, let's visit the homesteading example, as for a mom who wants to create an incredible homestead for their family you could tap into desires by saying something like:

> "Deep down inside, you would really love to be able to provide healthy, organic, homegrown food for your family. You imagine the day when you serve up a meal for your kids and you know that they're eating beautifully home grown fruits and vegetables from your

very own garden. You dream of having a sustainable farm-to-table lifestyle that gives you access to the most delicious, healthy food on this planet right outside the door of your kitchen."

It is the combination of speaking to your audience's pain and pleasure drivers that creates immense motivation for them to make a shift. The purpose of this is to reawaken the motivation that your audience has been pushing down or subduing in their life. When you do this, it unlocks in them a new level of commitment to move forward and make a change.

Uplevel Your Avatar

A mistake I notice many people make when choosing their target audience is focusing on trying to help people who don't have enough resources to pay for their services. This can be a hard realization because I know that your intention as a business owner is to help people and transform their lives. The problem is that if you focus on helping people who don't have resources to help themselves, you'll find it incredibly difficult to sell your products and services. Essentially, that type of market is great for a charity or nonprofit, but if you really want to grow a profitable business, choosing a target market that has resources will make your business growth much easier.

One of my clients recently discussed on a coaching call that she really wanted to help busy moms get control of their health. This is obviously a significant need in the marketplace; however, after discussion, we noticed that because she wanted to run a premium service, she had a lot of her audience saying they couldn't afford her services. We discussed the idea of upleveling her customer avatar. This essentially meant focusing on a similar target audience but adding the factor that they were professional moms struggling with their health. As soon as she started specifying her target audience was working professionals, she still attracted moms from all walks of life, but she also started to attract more people who had the resources to pay for her services.

As you consider your target market, I want you to ask yourself: do you need to uplevel who you're focusing on so that selling becomes easier? Here are some ways you can uplevel your customer avatar:

- One of the fastest ways is to focus on demographics with a higher level of income.
- Consider the different interests people with greater economic resources would have.
- Think about what magazines they read.
- Note what events they attend.
- Consider what cars they drive.
- Look at where they live.

When you start to think about this type of person, think about how they want to be spoken to. What words are they using when they describe their pain and their pleasures?

Feel Connected to Them

So far we've looked at being clear about the demographics for your target audience and examining their psychographics in terms of what drives their decision-making through pain and pleasure. One final thought I find really helpful is not just making up this data but choosing it from a real client.

There is something magical that happens when you don't just put data on a page and say that's your type of audience, but instead interview, connect with, and really experience your target audience.

I think it's a helpful exercise to spend time considering who your target audience could be and, once you're up and running, to be on the lookout for when you land a client who is that exact perfect audience. Something powerful happens when you think about a real person and the challenges they're actually having and the desires they have for their family and their lives. All of a sudden, it moves from clinical analysis into emotional resonance.

This means once you start speaking to them and creating marketing for them, you'll feel so much more connected to who they are and what they represent. This will ultimately lead to a greater sense of rapport with your audience and, ultimately, a more successful business.

Case Study Breakout: How Verena Tschudi Tripled Her Revenue

Verena is a career coach for female professionals who had developed an excellent program and built her coaching business over several years. Despite her expertise, she faced a common challenge—she lacked a strategic or automated marketing system that could consistently generate clients. While she would occasionally have a great month, the unpredictable nature of her business made it difficult to scale.

She decided to focus on designing one signature talk that she began delivering through online webinars. The breakthrough came when she realized she didn't need to create new content each time—she could deliver the same effective presentation repeatedly. This simple change transformed her business, and within 12 months, she had tripled her revenue.

When Verena initially joined our programs, she sent me a direct message stating that she was going to be one of our most successful students. What stands out about Verena is that she follows through on her commitments. She built her signature talk, delivered it consistently, and steadily grew her audience, which led to her first million-dollar year.

Today, Verena runs her business with a streamlined system that delivers results daily. But perhaps the most significant change isn't just the financial success—it's that she's no longer exhausted from running her business. She now has time for her family, connects with friends, and takes the vacations she'd previously put off. Her story shows how anyone with a driving desire to serve others and make a greater impact can create the life of their dreams.

Part III

Creating Your Signature Talk

Chapter 7

The Three Speaking Contexts

I had been asked to speak at a business mastermind workshop in Southern California. It was a group of about 15 entrepreneurs who were interested in selling from the stage. The leader of the group approached me and asked if I could share my expertise for an hour or so to help her mastermind members become more successful at selling from their webinars and in-person presentations.

In preparation for this event, I considered the challenges and opportunities these mastermind members faced. I spoke with the group leader and asked if it would be appropriate to make a unique offer for those who resonated with the content and wanted to work more deeply. The leader liked the idea of putting together something special for members who were serious about mastering this area.

When I walked into the room, it was light and bright, and people were obviously enjoying the experience. I spoke for about 60 minutes, and at the end, I shared a special offer I'd created just for the group. I handed out forms to the group members and said, "If you're interested in taking this offer, please give it to me or your leader by the end of the mastermind experience." A few people instantly gave me their forms and expressed their excitement about going deeper.

After answering some questions, I left feeling like the experience was a real win for all of us. Three days later, when the event had concluded, I received a text from the leader saying, "Are you ready for this?" I replied, "I'm not sure, but give it to me!" She responded, "Every single person, except for one who's in a unique situation, would like to take up your special offer."

That small mastermind workshop led to tens of thousands of dollars in income. I ended up getting to work with so many incredible entrepreneurs from just that one small event. Interestingly, I speak to many others in the industry who prefer not to do small speaking engagements because they don't get paid. For me, this is just one example of how, with the right strategy in place, every single speaking engagement can lead to clients—and often, many clients very quickly.

In this chapter, I want to break down the three types of presentations you'll be delivering. The good news is that all three essentially boil down to one signature presentation. The main difference is that each presentation will have a distinct ending: some will end with you getting a flood of clients, others will conclude with you collecting personal details for follow-up, and some will finish with a standing ovation. When done right, all of them will eventually generate revenue.

Selling from the stage can sometimes get a bad rap because people have had experiences where they felt they received no value and the speaker was only interested in making money. This can create a stigma around selling services from presentations. What you're going to learn through this process is that it can be done in a way that truly benefits everyone. In fact, I have spoken at events where I didn't make an offer, and the audience was actually disappointed that they didn't get a chance to buy something from me. They enjoyed the presentation and resonated with my content so much that they wanted to continue working with me, but because I didn't make an offer, they felt short-changed. This is amazing evidence that when you deliver your presentation the right way, your audience is in a buying mode and genuinely wants to invest in your expertise or services.

The Sharp Sell

The sharp sell is the name I've given to the talk that gets you paid right away. It's essentially the presentation you'll be delivering if you would like to make a direct offer at the end of your presentation. For example, if you are hosting your own webinar and would like to sell an online course at the end of your presentation and give people the opportunity to buy it right then and there, this would be called a *sharp sell*.

Remember, this is not a hard sell—it is a sharp sell. The goal is not for the audience to feel like you've done a hard close on them but to create an environment where the end of your presentation gets people to make a decision. The reason why I call it a sharp sell is because when you do it correctly, it truly penetrates the hearts and minds of your audience and gets them to commit to themselves on the next level.

What's really important to understand here is that a sharp sell is done only when you have full permission from the event organizer or if you are hosting the event yourself.

Let's explore some guidelines to consider for determining whether a sharp sell is the right presentation for your situation.

First, you need to have full permission to make the offer. If you're not speaking to your own audience, you need to ask permission from the event organizer and tell them about the offer you plan to make. Usually, if you are speaking at someone else's event, you may want to give them a commission from the sales. This way, it becomes a win for you, a win for them, and a win for the audience.

Second, if you are hosting an event for your own audience, you can obviously do a sharp sell because you don't need permission from anyone other than yourself. You have full permission to make an offer when and wherever you desire. This is why I always encourage my students to host their own virtual or in-person events. One of the easiest ways to get started with this is to host your own free virtual presentation. If you host your own 60- to 90-minute virtual presentation, there is very little cost to doing so, and it allows you to reach people from anywhere in the world. At the end of your presentation, if you create an offer that aligns with the content you've delivered and directly engages with your audience's desires, you'll make money.

The third important consideration is the offer you're making. The length of time you spend with the audience will impact the price point of your offer. If you are hosting a 60- to 90-minute webinar, I usually find that $2,000 and under is a great benchmark. You can always have higher-priced products and programs, but there should always be a price point that is $2,000 or less if you are speaking for 60–90 minutes. If you're offer is higher, then you'll want to use a soft sell, which we will discuss soon.

If you are hosting a multiday virtual event, you can feasibly pitch a direct offer of $10,000 and above. For in-person events, there really is no limit to the price point of the offer you can make, especially if it's a multiday experience. I've hosted in-person workshops that were three days long and had 40% of people take up a multi-five-figure offer.

Another question I frequently get about this type of presentation is "How many people should I expect to buy my program?" Obviously, that's like asking how long is a piece of string, because many elements factor into this: Is the offer irresistible? Does the content create desire for the offer? Finally, is the audience the right fit?

Assuming all these elements align, here are some good benchmarks based on virtual presentations for people who attend live:

- For a $2,000 offer: 5–10% conversion rate
- For a $1,000 offer: 10–15% conversion rate
- For a $297 offer: 10–20% or higher conversion rate

If you are hosting an in-person event, these conversion rates typically increase, and the price can increase also. I recommend the following as a benchmark for an in-person event:

- For a $2,000 offer: 30% conversion rate
- For a $5,000 offer: 20% or higher conversion rate
- For a $10,000+ offer: 10% or higher conversion rate

Obviously, these are just guidelines, and every situation and circumstance will differ, but they serve as good benchmarks to consider based on live attendance. Essentially, what I'm saying is that when someone is there live and actually hearing the offer, these conversion rates are good benchmarks to work from.

The Soft Sell

The *soft sell* is your signature talk that gets prospects' details in exchange for something valuable or books in a sales call as the follow-up. Not every time you speak will it be appropriate for you to make a direct offer for people to buy something then and there. There are many instances where the audience is seeing you for the first time, or the audience you're speaking to is not your own audience (meaning you are speaking at someone else's conference or event), and therefore making a direct offer is not appropriate (unless otherwise negotiated).

The Breakout Speaker

I was researching learning and development conferences and came across one particular conference that was offering breakout speakers. A breakout speaker is someone who doesn't speak on the main stage but offers a complementary workshop session as a specific stream option outside of the main keynote speakers. Although you don't get the notoriety from being a breakout speaker at conferences, in my opinion, there is more money to be made in the breakout rooms than on the main stage at these types of events.

I applied to be a breakout speaker and got approved. The conference had about 2,000 attendees, and my breakout room ended up having about 150 people. The good thing about a breakout session is that the people attending your session are choosing to be there. You usually have a very specific topic that they're interested in, and therefore, they show up with an intention of wanting to learn what you're sharing. Because of this, there tends to be more motivation in these rooms than even in the main keynote sessions.

I delivered my 60-minute presentation, and at the end, following the soft sell structure I made an offer to the audience to book in a free coaching session. At the time, I was doing a lot of corporate workshops and consulting (which I do almost none of now). My intention was to build trust with the people in the room, which would then lead to some coaching conversations with decision-makers in organizations, ideally leading to more work.

There was one particular person who really enjoyed my session, so much so that she wanted to bring me out to run a similar session for her clients. We ended up doing a coaching session together, and she paid for me to come out and deliver a workshop for some of her personal corporate clients. In that next workshop, there ended up being one person who was the learning and development director for a large company. That relationship turned into a six-figure corporate training opportunity.

As you can see, the flow-on effect in this instance was that I spoke for free at a conference where my target market attended. There was someone in the room who liked what I had to say, ended up booking a coaching session, and then shared me with their clients. That led to a very lucrative contract with a large corporation. This is a classic example of a soft sell presentation. I didn't make any direct offers during the presentation for people to buy something from me; however, in the presentation, I demonstrated that I had done specific types of work with different organizations and had seen great results.

If you want to do more work with organizations and large corporations, speaking in breakout rooms at industry conferences for free and then offering something valuable at the end is one of the most effective strategies for building trust and getting access to the inner circles of these big corporations with big budgets.

Masterclasses and Workshops

Another opportunity I had was when one of my good friends asked me to deliver a masterclass session for their large membership community. They wanted me to speak on "how to sell from webinars." The audience consisted mostly of online business owners, course creators, and small business owners—essentially my perfect target audience in my current business. This workshop was a free presentation where I could offer something useful and valuable at the end, where people could connect with me and go deeper into my content.

The cool thing about these opportunities is that when you can find entrepreneurs who have your target audience, there's a real win-win opportunity. You get to provide expertise and value for their community, the community receives amazing value, and this leads to high-quality leads coming into your world who are interested in buying your products. Many times, someone who has joined one of our Sell From Stage programs has reached out to me and said they first saw me in a free training inside a membership they were part of.

Speaking in other people's communities, group coaching programs, and masterminds is one of my favorite ways to add value, build a great reputation, and grow my business. When you think about it, the fact you're speaking in someone else's community means you have transferred trust from the community leader to you. They've essentially said you are the expert in this particular area and are trusted enough to come in and speak on that topic. The speed at which trust is built in this scenario is like lightning. If you do it the right way, this will lead to a lot of high-quality leads coming your way and ultimately a lot of sales on the back end.

High-Ticket Programs and High-Value Lead Magnets

As noted previously, a soft sell is mainly used in scenarios where making a direct offer is not allowed or not appropriate. This is usually when the audience you're speaking to is not your own audience—it's someone else's conference or community.

But you can also use the soft sell when the offer you want to make is a higher-ticket program.

For example, one of my previous students sells a program that is $8,000. Making a direct offer for an $8,000 program after spending only a short time together is a big ask. However, if someone watches your presentation, likes your content, style, and the value you've provided, and then you offer a free consultation to understand their business and give strategic direction along with options for working together, you can easily sell an $8,000 program.

A soft sell is great when you have a program that is usually $3,000 or more and you're spending only an hour or so with the audience in your presentation. We have seen a lot of success with students who simply run a 60-minute presentation and then offer a high-value consultation at the end for people interested in going deeper into the content and discussing next steps. Using this strategy can help sell programs anywhere between $3,000 and $50,000. There really are very few limits to this model.

You obviously need to understand how to deliver sales calls effectively, but the good thing is that most of the heavy lifting is done with the presentation. When people get on the call with you or your sales team, they're already in a high-trust situation because they've seen your presentation and know that you know how to help people. The call is really for them to understand whether their situation is a good fit for your program. That, my friend, is magic because it leads to high-converting sales with the right type of clients.

Similarly, you might simply offer a high-value PDF or worksheet that relates directly to the talk you delivered and the offer you have. For example, I get asked to talk a lot in communities about how to tell stories that sell. If I'm doing a soft sell presentation, I'll usually offer the community my "Sell With Story Guide." This is a short PDF that provides high value and gives people some tactical tools for building a story that sells.

If you create a high-value lead magnet that aligns with your topic and your offer, this is one of the most effective ways to flood your database with high-quality leads. My recommendation is to think about what offers you have and then consider creating a high-value PDF that aligns directly with that offer. You want to make sure not to overwhelm the audience with too many actions they need to take from the lead magnet, but you also want to provide enough value that they can see that your work is helpful and practical for them. From there, you can use email or any other marketing communication tactic that you have permission for to remarket to them, which will ultimately end up with them considering your program.

The No Sell

The *no sell* is the signature talk that gets you applause initially and then ultimately leads to clients. Think of your no sell talk as a classic keynote. The purpose of this presentation is to inspire the audience to make an internal decision to see a change in their life based on the topic you present. This type of presentation is usually delivered when you don't have permission to offer a lead magnet or make a direct offer. I'll usually do this presentation when I speak at larger conferences for other people's audiences.

One of my good friends, James Wedmore, asked me to speak at his conference called Business By Design. I was honored to be one of the keynote speakers, and the good news was that everyone in the audience was also in my target audience. At the time of this presentation, I was making a big pivot in my audience from delivering to corporate audiences to working with small business owners, coaches, and online course creators. Right around that time, I was also launching my beta version (which is essentially the first pilot program) of my flagship offer, Sell From Stage Academy®.

You need to remember this new Academy offer wasn't created yet, and I currently didn't have my own audience to sell it to. I just knew it was the right next step in my entrepreneurial journey. But as is usually the case when you make a decision to commit to something you believe in, opportunities show up for you. This opportunity to speak at the Business By Design conference was a perfect platform for me to build trust with a new audience.

I delivered my presentation for about 60 minutes and at the end told an emotive story that moved the audience to a standing ovation and loud cheers. I stepped off the stage and was happy with how the presentation went, but obviously no one had downloaded or bought anything from me. As I walked out to the main lobby area, I was flooded with a line of people who wanted to come up and thank me or ask questions.

One particular person, who was about third in the row, walked up to me and said, "Colin, that was such a powerful presentation. I feel like you really showed me how I can get clients using presentations. I don't know what you sell, but whatever it is, I want to buy it—here is my credit card." This was the moment that she literally put her physical credit card into my hands. We both exchanged some laughter, and I said to her I probably couldn't take her credit card, so I gave it back to her. But I did mention that I was running a new pilot program and gave her some details. She ended up signing up for that pilot program along with about 10 other people who were in the audience and asked about the programs that I offer. Those people who joined this initial beta program became so valuable to me because they were the first group of people in my new target audience who gave me encouragement, feedback, and some of the most incredible testimonials. This formed the foundation for my flagship online program.

To recap, a no sell presentation is delivered when you want to present a classic keynote style where there is no offer at the end. But if you do it right, following the strategies you'll learn in this book, it will lead to a flood of people wanting to inquire about your services.

Comparing the Endings

The three types of presentations I've just unpacked—the sharp sell, soft sell, and no sell—are essentially the same presentation but have slightly different endings:

- The sharp sell ends with you making a direct offer where someone can purchase from you right then and there
- The soft sell is where someone can book a high-value call or download a high-value resource in exchange for their personal details, and you'll then follow up with them and, if they're the right fit, sell them into your programs
- The no sell is your classic keynote with the goal of getting applause and a standing ovation at the end, but if you do it right, it leads to a line of people wanting to talk with you and work with you

These are the only three presentations you'll ever need, and the good news is that all three of these presentations cascade into one presentation, as they're essentially the same signature talk with different endings.

Chapter 8

Structuring Your Signature Talk

Your signature talk is the cornerstone for creating a sales system that gets you clients and grows your business. The signature talk could be a 60-minute presentation, two-hour workshop, or even a multiday event. For most of my clients, they like to focus on firstly building a 60-minute presentation that encapsulates everything you're learning in this book.

There are three main sections to building any signature talk:

- The first section is the opening. This is where you will connect with your audience and show them you care about what they're going through and you are the person to lead them.

- The second section will be the content. This is where you'll provide ideas that shift people's thinking and get them excited about the solution you help them with. You want to make sure you're still providing value in this section and not making it feel like a sales pitch.

- The third and final section is the close. This is where you offer the next step for the audience. This could be enrolling in your program, booking a consultation, or even simply downloading a valuable resource in exchange for their details.

Let me take you through in more detail what each of these sections entails so that you can even more deeply understand the process of building your signature talk.

The Opening

I was sitting in a small room with the leadership expert, John Maxwell. As he stood on the stage, he looked out into the audience. He didn't seem rushed; in fact, he was very calm and present. The room was full of successful entrepreneurs who were waiting to hear insights from his decades of leadership experience. As he looked out into the audience, his opening line was "Hi, I'm John, and I'm your friend."

There was something incredibly warm and inviting about his demeanor. In one simple statement John connected with our hearts. He showed his warmth and built trust with us almost instantly. John can use a statement like this because he is the number-one authority on leadership in the world, so the warmth he gives off is surprising because he carries so much authority. But I want you to capture the essence of what John did—he reached into our hearts and said that he cared.

There's an old saying: "People don't care how much you know until they know how much you care," and this principle rings true with the opening of your presentation. If you are doing a 60-minute talk, the first 10–15 minutes of that presentation need to show your audience that you understand who they are. You have to show them that you can lead them toward a more compelling future and also show them that you will share a path they too can follow if they choose. The essence of the opening is about touching people's hearts, and the purpose of touching their hearts is to connect with their personal challenges and desires.

I was doing a coaching session with an executive client who was presenting a case study at a large conference about strategies she had successfully implemented in her organization. She came to me with a very long document that outlined all the things she had done in her organization that had made a difference and the results achieved. Sure, the actions she took were inspiring—she'd gone into a lot of detail about why she took her approach and some of the challenges she had to overcome to see the cultural change and success they had achieved.

After hearing all of the information from her, I asked one question: "Who is this presentation about?"

Her answer was "Well, it's about me. It's about what I've done in our organization to achieve our success."

I looked at her with a compassionate heart and said, "I'm sorry, you're wrong. In fact, your presentation has nothing to do with you—it has everything to do with your audience."

She looked at me kind of puzzled at first because the presentation was a case study about things she had done. So I said to her, "If you get up there and present this content and talk about everything you know and what you've done, your audience will be bored out of their brains in the first five minutes and will leave remembering nothing. Is that the result you want?"

We laughed about this for a minute and she said, "No, I do not want that result."

So I said to her, "Let's make your presentation all about your audience." With that discussion, she started to change the way she introduced the topic. Instead of talking about the challenges she was facing in the organization, she started to bring up some of the challenges that not only she faced but also what other people are facing in the industry today. She spent some time exploring the difficulties that people in her industry face on a day-to-day basis when they're trying to make cultural changes. Then she started talking about the desires she had for her organization and reflected on the desires she had heard from other colleagues about how they wanted to see change in their organizations. After going through the challenges and the desires that she and other people in the industry experience, she asked people, "Who here resonates with this?" Everyone in the conference showed a gesture that they too experienced this.

Then, she went into clarifying the goal. Originally her goal was to present a breakdown of the strategy she used to see cultural change in her company, but after our conversation, she changed the goal to providing strategies and insights that every organization can use to see cultural success in the next 12 months. Her goal wasn't focused on herself; it was focused on how her audience could use the content she was about to share so that they could see a change in their situation.

In the opening lines of her presentation, initially she was just going to introduce herself, say who she was and the organization she was from, and outline why she was doing her presentation. But after realizing that her presentation wasn't about her but about her audience, she led with asking the audience some universal questions related to her topic. She asked:

- "Who here has ever struggled with changing the culture of their organization?"
- "Who here has ever had a desire to have less politics and more performance in their company?"
- "Who here would love some simple strategies that you can use to make your organization healthy and more profitable than ever before?"

She led with these three universal questions, and it set her apart in her presentation. The audience was instantly engaged and felt like she was there to connect with them rather than to just talk at them. You have to instantly show that you are there not to just share information and talk *at* your audience. You must show them you have spent the time to design a presentation that is for their benefit and is delivered in a way where it feels like a conversation instead of just a sharing of information.

In the opening section, you'll also want to share your signature story, or, as I call it, your conversion story. This is the story that showcases your journey from challenges to victory. It's the story that when you tell it, your audience sees themselves in the story and, once again, feels like you get them and you can lead them. You'll want your story to align, as closely as you can, with your core premise, which we explored in Chapter 4. It's also powerful to state your core premise in your opening so that your audience clearly understands the main idea your presentation is built upon.

That particular client saw me a month later and started smiling as I was walking toward her. I said, "What's up? You look happy." She laughed as she said, "Colin, after that presentation, not only did I get the highest ratings of the conference, but I had three job offers from other organizations." We both laughed, and I said jokingly, "You can't take those offers because your manager will never book me as a presentation coach again!" But that is the power of a great presentation that speaks deeply into the hearts of the audience.

Remember, the goal of the opening section of your presentation is to show your audience that you know what they're going through, you understand the challenges they are facing, and you hold dear the desires they too want for their life. You must also show them you are a leader that has achieved something in this field that they can aspire to. If you can do these things in the first 10–15 minutes of your presentation, you have won their hearts over, and they are one step closer to wanting to work with you or take whatever next step you have to offer.

The Content

There is a big difference between content that sells and content that tells. Many of us have been indoctrinated with content that tells the audience what they should do. If you have ever sat down to design a presentation to sell one of your programs, one of the first things you've probably done is gone into your course or program to find the most valuable content you have and thought, "If I can share this content with my audience for free and they see how valuable it is, then they will have a natural desire to want to buy something from me because they've already received so much value for free."

At the heart of this, there is a really good intention—to provide value for the audience up front so that you build trust with them, and ideally it leads to them wanting to work with you. The problem is that only part of this equation is true. In my real-life experience in coaching thousands of people and delivering hundreds of high-converting presentations, the best type of content not only provides high value but also creates high commitment from the audience.

When designing content for your presentation, you don't want to be thinking about creating content that impresses the audience with how smart you are. Most of the time, if you're trying to create content that shows your audience how brilliant and intelligent you are, you'll end up creating a presentation that confuses, overwhelms, and paralyzes your audience.

Remember, you are an expert in your field, and a lot of the time you don't realize how advanced your knowledge is compared to someone who is just beginning.

A great way to think about it is to imagine you were describing your content to a 10-year-old. You would have to present your content in a way that was clear, simple, but also compelling. If you've ever presented to young kids, you have to be very conscious of ensuring the content is engaging. As much as adults like to think of themselves as being highly sophisticated and highly disciplined, the truth is that many adults are just kids in grown-up bodies.

The first function of your ideas in the content section is to shift people's minds. What is that shift?, you might ask. The shift is from the resistance they experience about a particular topic to seeing it in a new perspective (we will get more in-depth into this in the coming chapters). It is to shift them from feeling interested in the topic to being committed to the topic, and it's also to shift them from looking at lots of options to get a result to choosing your main vehicle for getting the result they want.

The content section of your presentation in a 60-minute delivery will usually be anywhere between 30 and 40 minutes. Your content shouldn't be just teaching them the ideas from your program but should be built around changing how they view your topic. For example, one of our clients helps people transform their health by processing their unresolved emotions. Part of her content has to shift people's minds from seeing their health as being just physical to also being emotional. They have to show them that fixing your physical health is not always fixing the core issue—it's actually addressing the symptoms. For many people who have made all of the physical changes and are still not seeing health in their life, the core issue is many times unprocessed emotions that are being stored in the body and manifesting in physical symptoms.

This obviously is just an example and not my personal expertise, but you can see how if you are helping people process their emotions to create health in their life, there has to be a real psychological and perceptual shift that must occur for the audience to view processing their emotions as a valid vehicle for seeing true health in their life. So rather than just teaching how to process emotions, they have to show the audience a new way of viewing how they get a result.

I want you to think about what you help people with and ask yourself what shifts your audience needs to make mentally, emotionally, and even physically in order for them to view your offer from the right perspective. Your content should provide value but not just from a tactical perspective. You can always provide a little bit of tactical advice, but I find that an audience with a low commitment level—meaning they haven't paid money or have paid little money to enter the room—will get very overwhelmed by tactical advice quickly.

When you overwhelm your audience with tactical advice, what will happen is when it comes to making your offer, the audience will give you feedback like "This was really helpful. I'm going to do the actions you gave me already and see how they go, and then I'll try to come back three to six months from now and consider working with you." Can you see the problem here? The problem is that most of these people, or almost all of them, will never take the actions they're saying they will. Just because they have a good intention doesn't mean they're going to do it.

For example, have you ever had your brain picked? I know I have—it's painful. Usually, someone reaches out to you who has some sort of connection and asks if they can have a coffee with you and pick your brain. You say yes and go out to coffee with them. They drill you on all the information they want to know about your expertise and how they can get the result they want, and you give them everything. I mean, you let them drink from the fire hose. They thank you for your time (and you end up paying for the coffee), and you leave feeling like you really helped that person.

Two months later, you run into them randomly and ask how they've gone with the things you discussed. And this is what they say: "Yes, it was so helpful! I haven't had a chance to do anything yet, but I'll definitely get around to it in the future." By the way, that is code for "I'm never going to do it." This is what happens when you provide too much content during the content part of your presentation.

The second function of content should be some level of equipping their hands. As I mentioned, you have to be really careful with how much tactical advice you give during the content part of your presentation. You want to try to keep your presentation at a higher level, meaning focusing on stories, case studies, metaphors, and ideas, staying away from too many actions, tactics, and steps. If you do this, your audience will experience great value but also be ready to buy from you when you make your offer. It's okay to provide a little bit of tactical advice; for example, you could share one quick strategy they could use to get a result. But as I mentioned, you have to be really careful not to overwhelm your audience with too many how-to strategies as you just give them a to-do list that they will never do. Chapter 9 will explore in more depth the strategies for building content that connects and converts your audience into your programs, but I trust this is starting to lay the foundations for understanding the type of content you should be putting in and leaving out in your presentation.

The Close

I was sitting on my dining room floor with my soon-to-be wife planning our wedding. We didn't have much money, so most of the work we did was very manual. We had to design, cut out, and put together around 150 personal invitations for our guests. I remember sitting down with Sarah as we chose the fonts, paper, envelopes, and all the details of how we wanted to present the invitation. Most of the guests already knew they were invited to our wedding because we had mentioned it at some point, but this was the formal invitation. It was the invitation they were waiting for in anticipation. We had spent time, money, and a whole lot of effort preparing the formal process for inviting our guests to one of the most important days of our lives.

For me, when you close your presentation and make your offer, it is like a heartfelt invitation. It is the time and space where, after all the preparation and planning you've done, after delivering your content and connecting with your audience, you are formally inviting them to a special experience. For many people, when they think about selling from a stage, they think the close is some sort of heavy-handed, intense, and aggressive hard close. This is not how I want you to think about closing your presentation. I want you to think about it as a celebratory time where you invite the people who have really resonated with you and your content to commit to themselves on a greater level.

The close is the part of the presentation where you're asking your audience to take an action, to move their feet. If you've followed my process outlined in this book, you have touched their hearts through the opening, you have shifted their minds and equipped their hands in the content, and now you're asking them to move their feet.

Most people I speak with think that the close is the hardest part of the presentation because this is usually the section where you invite your audience to take the next step, whether that be to book a call, download a resource, or buy your program. Something I tell my students all the time is that if you haven't delivered the opening and the content effectively, the close will be ineffective.

Remember, the purpose of your entire presentation is to create an irresistible desire for people to want to work with you. If you put all of the weight of them buying your program on how well you close, it's going to feel like you have provided a bait and switch. The reason an audience can get upset when people close out their presentation with an offer to buy their program is because the expectations that were set during the presentation didn't align with the action the speaker is asking them to take at the end. Consider my wedding invitation example I shared at the start of the section: all of the guests already knew that they were going to be invited; they just hadn't received the formal invitation yet.

When you've built your presentation effectively and aligned everything toward the action you want them to take, the audience will feel like what you have to offer is something they really want to have. It's going to feel like the logical next step for them to take, and in fact, many times the audience will thank you for making such a great offer to them.

Once you've delivered your main content section, you're going to want to summarize everything you've covered. Don't go into too much detail here—you want to briefly cover the main points you spoke about in your content and be careful not to introduce any new concepts.

Amateurs make the mistake of adding new stories or concepts during the review of their presentation. From an audience

Structuring Your Signature Talk

perspective, this becomes overwhelming and feels like a waste of time. Once you've reviewed your content, you're going to want to move into some type of transition.

There are many types of transitions that I use and teach people. Let me give you one of the easiest ones you can use right away. After summarizing the key points of your presentation, your transition will be based on gaining assumed permission from the audience. Assumed permission is essentially asking a rhetorical question to gain permission.

A simple way you can do this is by first asking "Who here has resonated with me and the content today?" You're not necessarily asking for a verbal yes from the audience, but you can always ask people to raise their hands slightly or type the word "yes" in the chat if you're online. If you've done a good job in presenting useful content and engaging the audience throughout the presentation, you are going to get lots of yeses and agreements here.

Then you can say something like "For those people who have resonated today, would it be okay if I share with you what the next steps look like if you would like to implement this further with our help?"

After you've made this verbal transition, you can then go directly into your offer. If you're doing a soft sell, the offer will be to book a call with you or to download a valuable resource. If you are moving into a sharp sell, the offer will be to join one of your programs directly. During a sharp sell, you'll take the time to unpack your offer in a structured and well-paced manner. One of the secrets is not to rush through the offer but to take your time explaining how it works and how they can join it.

One technique I find that helps people feel more confident when making their offer is to imagine one of your most successful clients in your mind. As you transition out of your content into the close, picture that person who has seen amazing success and results, and think about how if you hadn't made this invitation to them, they would never have experienced that success. Remember, the goal is not to have everyone in the presentation say yes to your offer—the goal is to have the right people resonate with you and say a resounding yes when you make your invitation.

As you can see, the close of the presentation hinges so much on all the work that you've done previously. If you have done the previous work where you've understood who your audience is and what their challenges and desires are, built your presentation on your core premise, and created content that shifts the audience's thinking into the right perspective regarding your offer—then the close will come as a welcome experience for the audience. They will be excited to open up this envelope and join the special experience that you can share together.

Case Study Breakout: Jon Acampora's 3–14% Conversion Rate Increase

Jon had been delivering webinars for several years. He had built an online membership business, called Excel Campus, that helped professionals, usually in the finance field, to upskill themselves in Excel. Basically, he teaches people how to be good at spreadsheets so they can improve in their work, get noticed, and get promoted.

The problem Jon was having was that his presentations would get a lot of great comments and feedback but very low sales. He usually got around a 2–3% conversion rate on his live attendees during a webinar. He started implementing the

Sell From Stage formula, integrating his stories, content, and engagement in a totally new way. The first time he fully implemented the process, his conversion rate went from 3% to 14%. He ended up doing more than $80,000 in sales live on the webinar and got amazing feedback from the attendees.

Some of the big changes he made in his presentation was that he stopped teaching so much tactical or how-to content and started focusing on decision-based content that moved the audience to be more motivated toward their goals. He still provided high value during the presentation but didn't overwhelm them with too many things to do.

After the success of this presentation, he took that video and put it on an evergreen webinar platform. This is essentially where people can access a simulated live version of his presentation at any time they choose. The amazing thing was that his conversion rate still stayed extremely high. I remember texting him just over a year from when he first delivered this game-changing presentation and asking how much revenue it had generated since putting it on evergreen. He replied and said about $1.1 million, and then went on to say in his playful manner, "If an Excel nerd can make a million dollars with one presentation, then anyone can!"

Jon is a master at his craft—he is the market leader when it comes to teaching people Excel skills. However, designing the presentation to sell the skills he teaches is not necessarily his expertise. This is usually the case for many people: they are very good at their craft; however, they struggle to articulate the value of what they do for their audience.

Chapter 9

Selling Principles and Techniques

Now that you have reviewed the three main parts of a signature talk, let's explore in more detail the way in which you create high-converting content. What you're about to learn in this chapter are some powerful guiding principles for you to utilize when you're designing your content for your presentation. Many of my students have said that understanding these principles has fundamentally changed the way they think about content design. This has led to them becoming more persuasive presenters and building a presentation that gets them clients every time.

Decision-Based Content

For years, my wife and I discussed moving to the United States and seeing what we could do in that marketplace. Over that period, I would go on Google and discussion forums, take people out to coffee who had changed countries before, and essentially research how someone in my circumstances could successfully move to a new country.

The funny thing is that after three years of searching far and wide trying to understand "how" I could make this change, I realized I was more confused about how we were going to move from Australia to the United States than when I first started. I had so many conflicting pieces of advice and rhetoric that I felt paralyzed.

At that point, my wife and I made the decision that we definitely wanted to make the move. So we went out and hired an immigration attorney who showed us a five-step process that we could move through to relocate our lives and businesses overseas. The clarity that this immigration attorney gave us was incredible. All of a sudden, we could see a clear path ahead. We had paid them the money for the process to happen, and they laid out the steps they were going to take to hold our hand and achieve the result we wanted. Within about five months, our feet were on American soil.

I want you to get this: for three years, I researched how to change countries; however, in a matter of only a few months by making a decision to hire an expert and go through their process, we were quickly and surely able to achieve what we had been trying to achieve. The reason I share this story is because your audience thinks they need more information to see success, but the truth is they don't need more information—they need to make a decision.

In my scenario, I thought I needed more information, but because this information was coming from unqualified sources, it was creating more confusion and uncertainty in me. I didn't need more information; I needed to make a decision, which was cemented when I paid the invoice for the immigration attorney and they took me through a simple system for achieving what I desired.

Your audience is the same way. They're listening to your presentations thinking that they will get a result if they can just gather enough information. I do appreciate that information gathering is part of the decision-making process; however, if your presentation doesn't move the audience to a place of decision, essentially you are just leaving them in a perpetual cycle of researching.

So when you think about building content for your presentation, don't just think about how to teach people your knowledge. I want you to consider the question of how to present content that is both valuable but also motivates them to be more decisive. Some ways you can do this is through presenting case studies, asking powerful questions, and providing content that is clear and not overwhelming. These are just a few ways that you can move people out of information gathering into decision-making.

Reframe Their Resistances

Have you ever put your foot on the accelerator of your car only to realize the emergency or hand brake was still on? You know that feeling when you expect the car to take off but it feels as if something is grabbing it and holding it in place? That is what is happening in the minds and hearts of your prospects during your presentation. When they initially come into your presentation, they have a whole bunch of resistances and wrong beliefs that they have built up over the years that are stopping them from moving forward.

Many times, your prospects will think that the only thing stopping them from moving forward is that they don't know "how to do it," and if they only knew how to do it, then they would easily be able to move forward. With today's technology and information, knowing how to do something is readily available for almost everything. But I'm sure you'll agree that even after looking something up, a lot of times, you still don't do it.

For example, starting a business is readily available information on the Internet. You can look up either on Google or an AI and ask how to start a business. I'm sure you would get a 7- to 10-step plan that would show you the exact process for starting a business. But just because you've read the 7-step plan doesn't mean you're actually going to do it. The reason someone doesn't do something is usually not because they don't know how to do it—it's because they have some significant wrong beliefs or internal resistances that are stopping them from moving forward. Some of the most important content in your presentation has less to do with showing your audience how to do something and more to do with reframing the resistances that are stopping them from moving forward.

For example, in my topic of selling from a stage, there is an initial resistance where people have a misunderstanding of what selling is. Many people feel resistance when it comes to making an offer. You may feel this also—you might feel like selling something feels pushy and like you're trying to get someone to do something they don't want to do. Where does this belief come from? Usually, you've had experiences in your past where you got sold to, and it led to a decision that you regretted. You've also been exposed to thousands of books, movies, television shows, jokes, and anecdotes from friends and colleagues that portray people who are pitching something unsavory. So now, as an entrepreneur, when you think about selling your services, there is some internal dissonance that comes up, which is like having the emergency brake on your ability to offer your products. The truth is no one wants to be sold to, but everyone wants to buy something they desire.

In regard to the resistance I just mentioned, I'll usually reframe at the start of any presentation because if my prospects have a resistance to selling, they won't be able to take the next step even if they want to. The reframe I'll share is that you need to shift from seeing selling as pushy to seeing selling as serving. I covered this fairly in-depth in the early chapters, but to remind you, when selling is done with integrity, essentially it's really just helping your audience become more committed to their goals and providing them a solution for meeting those goals faster and more efficiently than if they were to do it by themselves. For our programs, if a student has a hang-up when it comes to selling, they're going to really struggle to implement the tactical strategies. So, the first reframe that needs to occur is that they need to create a new relationship with selling. I've had many students say to me that they write "selling is serving" on a sticky note and put it on the side of their computer as a reminder that when they sell, they're not doing the wrong thing—that when they sell to the right person, it creates opportunities, results, and transformation that never would have occurred previously.

Think about your topic and ask yourself the question, what resistances or misunderstandings do people have that stop them from moving forward? One of my students helps busy moms get back their energy and fitness in a way they've always dreamed of. One of the resistances she discovered was that they feel guilty about focusing on themselves when their family still has so many needs. So, at the start of her presentation, she began spending more time focusing on a reframe concept that helped her audience understand that through focusing on your own health, you are able to create family health because you can give only from what you have.

The metaphor she used is about putting on your own oxygen mask, as instructed by flight attendants before you put on the oxygen masks of anyone else. When you create health and energy in your own body, you can far more effectively serve and help those people around you who mean the most to you. Can you see how if she didn't address this resistance in her audience, it doesn't matter how good her offer is or how much tactical information she gives them? They won't move forward because there is a fundamental belief that the audience currently has: "I shouldn't be looking after myself; I should be looking after everyone else."

One of the secrets to reframing beliefs is using metaphors. Metaphors are one of the most powerful linguistic tools you have because they are vague enough for people to understand but allow for meaning and interpretation to change. The example of using the metaphor of putting your oxygen mask on first is a really effective metaphor for the reframe. Metaphors help your audience to understand the concept and can also be powerful in reframing concepts. I'm not sure if you noticed, but I started this section with the metaphor of internal resistance being like having the emergency or handbrake on while you try to accelerate. It doesn't matter how much acceleration you have—if the brake is on, the car is going nowhere. That is an example of how metaphor helps people understand concepts and prepares them for or creates a reframe. The goal of this chapter is to help you identify those brakes and start to release them.

One of my students, Megan Walker, helps health and medical practitioners who provide one-to-one services to start serving and scaling up their practice through online education platforms. She has an incredible coaching program that has helped many health professionals put their knowledge together and provide more resources to their clients without doing any extra work. The problem she faced was that health professionals were very much trained in a traditional model through college. They were trained that the service they give should always involve having the patient and the practitioner in the same room working one-on-one.

While this might be the case for some of their patients, there will be many patients who would also love to do some online work about their specific topic. For example, let's say they are a physiotherapist—after an initial consultation, they can refer patients to the online program for comprehensive movement and stretch management processes. So the reframe here is that as a health practitioner, you can transform more lives by not being in the room. Another way of saying it is that you can reach more people and make more of an impact by productizing your knowledge and making it available to your patients. This shift in thinking needs to occur first before she can really help them build and productize their knowledge. I hope you can see that it doesn't matter how much tactical information she gave them—if the health practitioner believes that the only way of working with a patient is being present in the room with them one-on-one, then they will never implement the transformation process she has for them.

So I want you to consider: What are the resistances for your audience? What are the hangups or misunderstandings that your audience has about the topic that you teach? This needs to be a key part of your presentation because it will help to release the emergency brakes, which is the real reason why they haven't moved forward.

Entice Their Desires

I was never deeply interested in watches. I remember owning a few watches like Casio and Citizen, and sure, I liked wearing them, but they were definitely not a passion. This was until I met my friend Darren. Darren started educating me on the history of some of the more iconic watches. He told me about the movements that different watchmakers used and the complications and thousands of hours that went into each timepiece. After a period of time being friends with Darren, I also started having a passion for watches. This passion eventually came to a point where I started buying expensive watches (yes, I became that guy).

If I look back over my journey of this very expensive hobby, it's interesting to reflect on the fact that when I started, I had some interest in watches, but it wasn't until I started to understand the history, meaning, and nuances that I developed a passion that led to me walking into a watch store and purchasing a timepiece. If you had asked me several years before I met Darren if I would spend a lot of money on a watch, I would say no. Ask me now, and it's not even a question; I just know that I want it. My wife is someone who loves spending money on experiences like vacations, movies, and trips, which is why I jokingly say to her that my watch is an "experience" that I get to have every day! The transformation that I went through in my relationship and passion for watches is similar to the transformation that you have to take people on—moving their desires from being interested to being passionate and committed.

One of the secrets to selling more of your products and programs is creating content that increases the desire for your audience to commit to the result they want. So often, when your audience gets on a presentation and starts listening to you, their commitment level is a lot lower than they realize. The very fact that they're listening to you live or watching a recorded presentation shows that they at least have an interest in the topic, but there's a big difference between them having an interest and pulling out their credit card to spend a couple of thousand dollars after an hour or so with you.

How do you move someone from being interested to being incredibly committed? One of my favorite ways to do this is to consider the most interesting or desirable topic that sits within all of the topics that you teach. For me, one of the most desirable topics that people want to understand in what I teach is storytelling. So, storytelling is going to be a big part of my presentation when I'm building a presentation to sell.

One of my students helps corporate professionals get promotions, and one of the most desirable topics in this area is how to ask your boss for a raise. So, she will have that piece of content in her presentation because it's a really desirable part of what she teaches. But here's the secret that most people don't understand: you need to present the topic in a way that creates a greater desire for the audience to want to learn, as opposed to teaching them absolutely everything that you know about the topic. You don't want them finishing the presentation and feeling like they know everything they need to know and therefore don't need your program.

Using the example of teaching people how to ask their boss for a raise, some ways you could approach that include sharing stories of previous students who have successfully asked for a raise and the journey they went on, both internally and externally. Sharing stories or case studies of previous people who have gone through it doesn't necessarily show someone how to do it, but it helps the audience understand the types of people and the challenges and opportunities they have moved through to create their promotion.

You could also share a high-level framework that shows the process of building toward a promotion, which could be: (1) Identifying the job you want, (2) finding the decision-maker, (3) compiling your promotion pack, (4) having the conversation, (5) and following up effectively. By the way, I just made up that process. But as you can see, that five-step process makes sense and also doesn't give away all of the nitty-gritty actions one must take to complete the process. In your presentation, you might go a little bit deeper into step 4. Having the conversation, but even just showing the audience that there are five big steps will help them realize that they don't understand everything.

Another thing you can do with this teaching point is to share some questions people should ask themselves before going into the conversation. Rather than giving people the exact scripts and templates to have the conversation, you want to provide enough information that the listener genuinely feels like they have a better understanding but doesn't feel like they can just do it themselves.

One thing to remember here is that many times your audience hasn't gotten results, not because they don't have the tactical tools but because they don't have the support or accountability they need. That is one element they will receive when they join your program that they don't get without you. Maybe then, in your coaching programs or masterminds, more than half the value is just being in the group. So you don't need to feel bad about not giving people absolutely everything in a free presentation. You need to provide enough value that the listeners genuinely feel like they've gained more clarity and were able to identify some motivation factors, but you don't want to overwhelm them with so much information that they feel like they have six months of work before they should even consider joining a program.

When you teach in a way that creates desire for a topic as opposed to teaching everything they need to know, it increases motivation. The one thing that your audience really needs is a greater level of motivation and commitment toward the topic. All transformations happen through making a decision. So, you have to teach in a way that increases people's desires as opposed to quenching them. When you think about it, part of your teaching should be about reframing people's resistances, which we talked about in the previous section; then you need to teach some content that is really interesting to the audience but doesn't quench all of their questions and desires on the topic. It still leaves an open loop or a desire for them to learn more. It increases their commitment to the topic instead of overwhelming them with 37 action items after they finish the presentation with you. A high-converting presentation leaves the audience with one thing to do, which is to decide if they want to join your program or continue the journey on their own.

Reveal the Vehicle

After you've removed their resistances and increased their desire to learn more, the final reason someone will join your program is because you can show them a clear, compelling, and powerful way to get them the result that they desire. The way that you get someone a result is through your vehicle. We talked a lot about the vehicle in the core premise chapter, but as a reminder, your vehicle is the way in which you get someone a result.

For example, my vehicle is building a high-converting presentation. However, there are many types of vehicles. I have lots of clients who are life and spiritual coaches and therefore the vehicle that they use to get results can be owning a new identity, manifestation, or even self-coaching.

I also have a lot of clients who teach people how to generate leads in their business. The way in which they do that varies significantly—for some, the vehicle is using Facebook groups; for others, it's through building a personal brand; for others, it's through YouTube ads; and for others, it's through organic social media. As you can see, the vehicle that you choose doesn't have to be anything special, but it does need to be clear and concise so that the audience understands that you are going to teach them a way to get the outcome they're looking for.

Here's where the special sauce comes in: you need to present your vehicle in a way that is unique, clear, and compelling. You need to show your vehicle in a way that when the audience sees and hears it, they can see a path through which they can achieve their result. One of the easiest ways to do this is to break down your vehicle or methodology into three to seven big steps.

For example, if you were teaching Facebook groups as your way of helping people generate high-quality leads that turn into high-paying clients, you could present your Facebook group methodology as a four-phased process:

1. **Identify:** Identify your dream audience.
2. **Build:** Create a Facebook group with your specific audience in mind.
3. **Invite:** Build an invitation system that grows the Facebook group.
4. **Convert:** Create an engaged community using invitational posts that lead to sales.

I just made up this process, but I bet that if I were presenting to you a Facebook lead generation system that followed those four big pillars and I could show you that you could generate high-quality leads at a really low cost for your business, you would be interested in going deeper into this methodology. As long as it was focused on the goal you had and aligned with your own personal values, this type of methodology would sell.

In fact, I know for certain that there are people teaching Facebook group lead generation methodology that have a lot of success in the marketplace.

Maybe you're a life coach, and you teach people how to break free from the emotional trauma that stops them from being fully confident in themselves. So essentially, the vehicle is resolving emotional trauma, but how you present it can be unique to you. For example, you could have a three-step formula:

1. Discovering emotional triggers

2. Resolving internal trauma

3. Stepping into your new identity

This three-step process makes sense for people, and it also doesn't go into too much detail. It will create curiosity and intrigue without overwhelming them with too many things to do right away. Obviously, when someone joins your program or course, they should be given every single step, framework, and structure they need to achieve the result that you promised. But when you are initially presenting your vehicle, you want to make sure not to overwhelm your audience with too much detail; if you do make this mistake, you will slow down the sales process.

A great way of thinking about your vehicle is asking yourself what are the three to seven big pillars that you teach that lead to someone getting a transformation. These can be put in a linear ordered fashion, or they can also be shown in a non-linear modular fashion. As long as when an audience hears you describe the process, it is clear and makes sense to their minds, then they will see themselves using those big pillars to achieve the result they want.

As I mentioned, one of the big mistakes people make is getting into too much detail within each of the pillars. This is usually because you're really excited about the process you take people through. The problem is that your listeners are far less committed to the outcome than you realize. They haven't put money or skin in the game yet—they're really just trying to understand what the big process is that you can take them through to achieve their desired results.

Usually, the simpler the process, the better. So often, I've seen students present their vehicle and it has 9 or 12 steps involved. In my experience, this is way too many—I usually recommend anywhere between 3 to 7 steps at the most. Remember, when someone gets into your program, you can show them that within each of these steps there are another 7 steps they need to move through to achieve just one of the pillars. That is totally fine. The problem is that when you're trying to sell something and you're showing it in an overly complex manner, you are going to repel the very audience that you desperately want to serve.

Share Powerful Stories

Storytelling is one of the secrets to becoming a masterful communicator. *New York Times* bestselling author and social media maverick Gary Vaynerchuk said, "Storytelling is by far the most underrated skill when it comes to business." And it was Plato who said "Those who tell stories rule society."

Storytelling is one of those soft skills that can easily be overlooked; however, when honed and harnessed effectively, it is one of the most valuable speaking and sales skills you'll ever learn. One of the challenges when it comes to storytelling is that you may believe you aren't a good storyteller.

You might feel like your stories are boring or that you don't have any stories to tell. I've worked with thousands of clients, and let me tell you this: you have a story. In fact, every single person I know has a story, and when you discover that story and tell it effectively, it will connect with your audience and naturally draw them toward wanting to work with you.

The reason stories are so powerful is that they move past the conscious mind and awaken the unconscious mind. I have two young kids, and when they were getting ready to go to sleep, they would always ask me to tell them a story. If you're a parent, you've probably had to tell many stories to your kids. That magical sentence "Once upon a time" opens up the curious hearts of our children, but it also opens the hearts and minds of adults. In fact, I believe that when we tell stories, we're essentially tapping into the childlike aspects of who we are, which is based around curiosity, openness, and tenderness.

This is powerful from a sales perspective because all of the objections and resistances that your audience has toward your program are found in the conscious mind. It is the unconscious mind that ultimately guides gut-based decisions. So, if you have the power to have some influence on the unconscious mind, you have ultimate power in your persuasion. Obviously, you have to use stories with integrity, and your product has to deliver what it says it delivers. I'm going to assume that your product and program are exceptional, and therefore the use of stories is integral in attracting the right audience to your programs.

I was standing on my lunch break during a workshop eating a ham and cheese sandwich. My mentor at the time came up to me and asked how my coaching business was going. I told her, "It's going incredible; I love asking questions and having conversations with people." She smiled and said, "That's

Selling Principles and Techniques

fantastic," and then she asked me, "How much money are you making right now?"

I was taken aback by the question because I didn't expect her to be so up front with this topic. But I think the main reason I was taken aback was that at the time I wasn't making much money. In fact, I was making about $250 per month. So I said to her, "I'm making about $250 per month."

As soon as I said that number, her face changed. She looked me in the eyes, and she said, "Colin, you've got such great support here in the coaching school, you're developing a great skill set, and you believe in what you do." Then she said, "You want to have kids, right?" I said, "Yeah, I really do." And she said, "You know what? Three years from now you'll probably have kids, but if we're honest, they won't have anything to look up to. Do you know what I think you are, Colin? You're a schmuck. You've let your fear and your stories get in the way of your plan and your purpose."

It was in that moment that I realized that a piece of ham had fallen out of the sandwich and was now sitting on my foot, and all of the blood had drained from my face. But I also realized that what she said was true—I was letting my limiting stories be the loudest voices in my life.

Then she went on to say, "I want you to go out and make $30,000 over the next three months and call me personally. Here's my number." This motivated me at such a deep level that I made a decision that I wasn't going to let my limiting stories stop me from going after my compelling future anymore.

Over the next three months, I took courageous action, and at the end of it, while doing my finances, I realized that I had actually made more than $30,000 over that three-month period. I called up my mentor and I said, "You wouldn't believe it, I achieved the goal that you set me." And she said, "I do believe it.

In fact, you always had it within you; you were just living from fear instead of courage. Well done."

This is a personal story for me, but it's also one that I will share in different presentations when I want to reinforce the fact that all of us let our fears get in the way of our faith at different points in our life. As you read that story, I wonder what came up for you? Did you start thinking about your own limiting beliefs and your own fears even as I was talking about my story? That, my friend, is the power of telling great stories. When you tell a story, you not only share your story, but you also speak to the unconscious mind of the audience, and it reveals their own story.

There are many types of stories that you can share in your presentations, but for me there are really only two purposes of stories. The first purpose is to reinforce the core premise. If you recall, I started the book talking about the idea of a core premise, which is the one idea that, when the audience accepts it, would make your offer the logical next step. Finding a story that reinforces your core premise is one of the secrets to selling without selling—this is what I refer to as your conversion story.

The second purpose of a story is one that simply reinforces one of the key ideas that you're sharing in your signature talk. You usually have between three to five key ideas and concepts, and you'll want to have a story for most of those ideas. This can be a personal story or a client story. What's most important is that you do share a story. I've found that the majority of my clients, when they start working with our programs, say they realize they haven't shared enough stories. I think there's a belief out there that in business you don't really need to share stories—that on some level, stories are not appropriate for a business context. But in my experience, it's your stories that will differentiate you from anyone else in the marketplace.

Selling Principles and Techniques

One of my students, Megan Sumrell, who runs a company called The Pink Bee, shared with me that before using my Sell From Stage formulas, she would really struggle to make sales in her planning and time management programs for women. She had a massive heart to help women who were overwhelmed and overworked to feel back in control of their lives, and she had amazing tools and strategies to help them; however, she struggled to convert her ideal prospects into her programs.

Previously, she would use a lot of statistics and tactical ideas in her presentations and talk a lot about her corporate work. This led to some really nice comments on her webinars but very few conversions. Everything changed when she started to implement storytelling more effectively within her signature talks. Previously, a lot of her stories would be around her corporate career and how she used her strategies to become more productive.

When she understood the power of storytelling and the idea of bringing in more emotion and personalizing her stories, she changed her approach. The story she now shared was about being at the park with her daughter, pushing her on the swing, when another mom standing next to her struck up a conversation. They had a general discussion about their daughters and their lives, and then the other mom asked her, "What do you do for fun?"

Megan paused and thought deeply. It was at that moment she realized that she had forgotten what she did for fun. In fact, she'd built her life, without knowing it, into a place where she really wasn't enjoying much of what she was doing. She'd lost her sense of self in the midst of all her responsibilities. It was in that moment that she decided she needed to reprioritize her life and rediscover what was important to her and what really filled her up personally. That decision led to redesigning a life where she was not only there for others but also there for herself. She realized she needed a better priority and planning system so that she could live the life she'd always desired. This story is a really great example of someone who has a very left-brain topic—planning and productivity—and brought in an emotive right-brain experience that shares the core premise of her work but also links it to the heart of her ideal audience.

When did you experience one of those defining moments in your life? Think back over your life and consider some of the more meaningful or transformational moments that have shaped who you are today. Those moments don't need to be highly dramatic—they can be small conversations or they could be traumatic situations. Either way, it was those moments that shaped who you are and the trajectory of your life.

If you can consider the more meaningful moments in your life where you made some of your significant decisions, you'll discover your most powerful stories. When I'm designing a presentation, I usually start with my key ideas. Then I look at these key ideas and ask: When have I had a personal experience with these concepts? When have I experienced a transformation or been impacted by this concept in my life? I then write down these stories, and they form the fabric for the emotive engagement in my signature talk.

Case Study Breakout: Marco Bernard's $3,000–$140,000 Presentation Shift

Marco is a French podcasting expert. Essentially, he helps French-speaking individuals launch, grow, and scale their podcasts. When he first came to me, he had already been running a few webinars. The most he had ever made in a webinar was $3,000. He had a real passion for helping his audience and knew there was an opportunity in the market as there were very few people helping the French-speaking community grow their podcasts. He had personally experienced a transformation by launching his podcast, as it helped him grow his profile, his audience, and his business.

He knew that he wanted to use webinars more often to launch his signature product, but the problem was every single time he did it, he kept getting the same results. He'd make a few thousand dollars, and it really wasn't enough for him to go full-time in his business, especially having a young family.

He made some big changes to his webinar presentation using my Sell From Stage strategies, which included:

- Sharing his conversion story at the start of his presentation
- Changing the way he delivered his concepts to focus more on increasing desire and reducing resistance
- Stopping the practice of just teaching the content from his course
- Thinking more strategically about his offer and the type of content needed in his presentation for the audience to make a decision to join

After he made these changes, he went from a $3,000 webinar to a $47,144 webinar—essentially more than 15× his results. The cool thing was that he went on from there and started implementing this presentation over and over again, growing his audience each time. The following year he did five launches and made $57,742; $81,406; $54,778; $81,167; and $71,029. As you can see, through this one presentation, he was able to deliver it repeatedly and start getting consistent results.

Then in the following year, he posted in our members group sharing that he had run his first $158,453 webinar. He's gone on to build a million-dollar coaching business helping French online educators and coaches launch and grow their podcasts. The thing I love about Marco is his commitment to his students and to his mission. He's had many challenges along the way, as all of us do in growing a business, but he stayed focused and consistent in doing what works. The result has been that in about a three-year period, he was able to go from making only a few thousand dollars a year to making over a million.

It's stories like this that remind me of the reason why I do this work—to help people just like Marco access their dreams and impact people in a way that I could have never reached myself.

Chapter 10

The Pitch

By this point, you have connected with your audience and shown them that you not only understand them but can lead them. You've delivered content that has reframed the resistances, ignited their desire to want to learn more, and shown them that there is a clear path ahead that they can follow. Now it is your time to invite them to take the next step.

For many people, they get really nervous when it comes to offering their program. Most of the time that's because you feel like you're transitioning out of providing a lot of valuable information into just simply asking them to give you money. I want you to think about your pitch as simply making an invitation. You have prepared the room, and you are inviting them to take the next step toward achieving their goals faster and more efficiently with your help. Your help won't be a perfect fit for everyone, but for those who resonate with you and want to achieve what your program can give them, it will be a transformative experience.

Access Your Certainty

The first thing that people buy isn't your program; it's a feeling. Before they buy any products from you, essentially what they are looking for is a feeling of certainty. Your audience is experiencing a lot of uncertainty in the particular area you can help them with. Let's say you help people lose weight and regain their health—they are sitting in the audience listening to your presentation feeling uncertain and confused about how they can achieve their health goals. If you help people get leads for their business, they are sitting in the audience feeling confused and uncertain about where their next lead is coming from.

If you as the speaker are giving off an emotion of fear and uncertainty yourself, the audience will pick that up unconsciously. They are secretly looking to be led by you. Remember, most people don't want to make scary decisions for their lives, so you represent a safety boat for them to get across uncharted waters.

For example, have you ever bought something from someone and after you made the transaction, you thought to yourself, "I'm not even sure how this service works, but I just feel like they know what they are talking about and can help me." That is a classic example of you buying a feeling of certainty from a service provider. This is not a bad thing—this is a human thing. We as humans are constantly looking for a sense of certainty, and when you represent that sense of certainty to your prospects, it will increase sales dramatically.

But, you might be thinking, "How on Earth can I feel confident when I'm making an offer?" There are three ways of feeling confident when you make your offer: perspective, practice, and proof. I put them in that order for a reason because if you're just getting started, you won't have a whole lot of proof, but you can always change your perspective.

The first secret to feeling certain when you pitch your offer is to take on a perspective of service. One of the mistakes that people make when it comes to selling is they slip into the mindset of feeling like they are just asking their audience for money. If you start thinking of selling as asking your audience for money, you'll feel nervous and fearful because the whole energy behind that is you're taking something from someone.

I want you to completely flip this and see making your offer as an act of service. One of the best ways to do this is to think about how your intention of creating the offer is to help people achieve a result that they could not have achieved by themselves. Remember when we talked about your offer being a sacred place of transformation. Energetically, I want you to think about the offer as a place you are protecting, not something you are trying to push someone into doing. Your goal is to present your offer from an energetic space of helping people get a transformation.

Something that also helps through this process can be simply thinking about the impact that the product or process you teach has had on your own personal life. This for me was one of the most helpful perspectives when I was first getting started because I didn't have many clients, but I did know that the service I was offering had an impact on my life. When I was first a life coach, I had experienced personally the power of coaching sessions, and I could use that experience as fuel and enthusiasm for wanting to share this with other people.

The second way to get confident is to practice making your offer. The first time I make any type of offer, I always practice it in front of the mirror at least 10 or more times out loud. Part of feeling confident is simply allowing your body to say the words that you want it to say. The first couple of times that you make your pitch out loud, you'll feel all of the nervous energy in your body. After several times that nervous energy will start to subside and what will be replaced is a sense of calmness and familiarity.

One of the things I tell my clients when they are raising their prices is to practice saying it in the mirror out loud as if you're saying it to a client 10 or more times. At the start, it will feel clunky and unnerving, but by the end, it will be a normal part of your language set. Practicing making your offer goes a long way to increase your confidence. It's like anything—if you practice it more, you become more confident in it.

You don't want to be heading into your pitch and going through the process for the first time. It should feel like something that is extremely familiar and somewhat second nature because you've practiced it enough times. A lot of the time people misunderstand the meaning of their lack of confidence—they think that because they don't feel confident it means they can't do it, but the truth is that it simply means you are unfamiliar with the process, and so as you become familiar with it, your confidence will grow.

The final thing that will help with your confidence is gaining more proof that your product helps people. If you have any testimonials, I encourage you to read through those testimonials regularly, especially before you do a pitch in your presentation. I personally have a whole photo album set aside for client testimonials. Often people in our community will post their business wins, send me direct messages via social media, and also send formal written and video testimonials. I capture all of these in one place on my phone and regularly revisit them to remind me of how powerful the process is for people when they implement it.

A technique that I've mentioned previously but is worth revisiting is picturing a real client or person you know you've helped. Imagine them in their home environment or wherever you normally help them, and imagine their struggles before working with you. Now think about the joy that your solutions have brought to their life because it has alleviated much or almost all of that pain. It has replaced it with a sense of freedom and purpose in life that they hadn't experienced before. Imagining a real person in your mind and really connecting with the emotions of how your product helped them will do wonders in elevating your certainty.

Building your confidence muscle is extremely important as you learn to become a powerful leader for your clients. Keep your focus on a sense of service for your audience, practice your pitch multiple times, and remind yourself regularly that you're making an impact. This will all go a long way in increasing your certainty, which is the first thing people buy from you.

Follow a Formula

My wife asked me to make her a cake for her birthday. So as a good husband, I was up for the challenge. The problem was that I'd never baked a cake before. Imagine I went up to my local store and just purchased a bunch of random ingredients based on what I thought might be in a cake. Imagine me walking down the aisles telling myself "I need to make a cake" and then grabbing some sugar, flour, salt, eggs, cream, etc., and bringing it home. I get the ingredients out and start mixing them together, just making up in my head how much each ingredient should be in the cake. Then I put the cake in to bake and cross my fingers. How well do you think this cake is going to go? More importantly, how many husband points do you think I'm going to get? I'm going to score pretty low on the husband point factor—I might get some good intention points, but that's about it.

Thankfully, I didn't just do any guesswork. I went into the supermarket and got a pre-made cake mix. It told me exactly what ingredients I needed to put in to make the cake. It was the first time I'd ever made a cake, and after I followed the ingredients process, I was pretty happy with the result. The cake turned out great, my wife was happy, and I scored some killer husband points.

The problem is that most people don't follow any formulas when they pitch their programs. They essentially just make up what they believe should be in it and hope for the best. Obviously, depending on your product or program, there will be a slightly different formula, but I'd love to share with you some general guidelines that will help to structure your pitch so that your audience joins your programs.

After you finish the content of your presentation, you'll usually summarize the presentation and do your transition. After you've transitioned, you'll move into your pitch. You don't need to overthink this, but you do need to structure it in a way that makes logical sense and creates emotional buy-in.

Here is the general flow that you can follow, though obviously you can adjust it to what makes sense for you and what feels good during the presentation:

1. Include the name of your product. Don't spend too much time explaining why you named the product what you did, as your prospects don't really care—they only care that the name is clear and compelling.

2. Share why you built the product. Your prospects do care about your intention behind the product. Your reason should address the problem they're facing and be focused on the solution. Give a reason like "I noticed that people were struggling with this, so I want to help people create this result."

3. Be clear about who the product is for. This can be as simple as describing the categories of people who use it.

4. Take people through the main sections of your program. Remember, this should be kept to three to seven sections. Anything more than that will be too overwhelming for your audience. Talk about the outcome of each section as opposed to all the detail within it.

5. Include special bonuses. The purpose of having bonuses is to highlight parts of your program that either are most exciting or address specific objections people have.

6. Review the program overall and provide the total value. In other words, if someone was to implement your program, what sort of value could this add to their life or business?

7. Share the actual price they will pay for the program and any payment plans that are available.

8. Include one to three short testimonials from people based on the results they've achieved.

9. Show people how they can join your program by visiting a specific website or completing a certain form.

10. Include a fast-acting bonus that rewards people who take action by a certain time. This could be a special bonus for people who join during the presentation or in the first 24 hours after.

11. Answer questions about the offer. Always have between three and five prepared frequently asked questions. The purpose of answering these questions is to handle any final objections people have.

As you can see, there are quite a few elements to the pitch. The most important things to keep in mind are to pace yourself through the process, keep it focused on the results people are going to get rather than all the detail within your offer, and maintain the intention that you are there to serve them toward a transformation they really desire.

Pace Yourself

So often people will say to me that when they're doing a presentation, all of the content feels amazing and they're in such high spirits, but as soon as they transition into the pitch, the cool vibes go to zero. It's like everyone is having a party in the classroom and then all of a sudden the principal walks in and the party stops.

One of the common mistakes I notice people make when they pitch their programs is they skip through the offer too fast. I notice they spend a lot of time going through their content at the beginning of their presentation and teach with a sense of confidence and contribution. But as soon as they transition into their offer, they tend to skip through it as if they're ashamed of it. They are taking their time in the content part of their presentation, telling amazing stories and metaphors, and then they get to the pitch and skip through the slides, and the whole energy changes.

Something really important to keep in mind when you get into your pitch is to pace yourself. Don't skip through the offer as if it's something you're trying to avoid talking about. If you've done a great presentation at the front end, you've earned the right to talk about the next steps for those people who resonate with you.

One thing that can really help with this is designing a slide deck that takes people through your pitch. I personally like using simple slides that outline the main ideas and have powerful imagery. We provide slide decks to our students, showing them the style of slides that work best so that they don't overwhelm their audience during the pitch, but you can always build them yourself using any type of slide creation platform. The challenge here is trying to get the right balance of detail. Remember, the goal is not to overwhelm people with too much but to give them enough clarity that they feel a sense of certainty. I usually find that creating simple slides that have the outcome of each section of your offer works well. For example, if you have five sections in your program, sharing the name of each section and its outcome is a nice balance. You don't need to get bogged down in the details of every single thing that you do within your program.

Remember, the main thing that the prospect wants is a result. As much as you're really excited about all of your steps and processes, to the prospect, all that represents is more work to do. So when you are pitching your program, you want to make sure you're more focused on the result that each part of your program gives, as opposed to all the steps that the person has to take to get that result.

Give yourself permission to pace yourself when you're doing your pitch because what you'll find is that the people who are really interested in your offer genuinely want you to explain how it works and what they can get out of it. If you've done your presentation right, the prospects who are still listening to your presentation are at a crossroads in their life, and this decision for them is an important one for their future.

When you don't take the time to explain your offer properly or skip through it as many people do, you're not respecting the important decision-making process that your prospects are processing. Sure, there will always be a few people in your audience who don't feel like the offer is for them, but the interesting thing is that many of them will still be interested in learning about the offer.

Take your time and pace yourself when you make your pitch, and your audience—and your bank account—will thank you later.

Handle Questions as Objections

As you close out your presentation, you want to make sure that you answer any questions people have before they can make their decision to join your program. It's a good idea to prepare five to seven questions that your audience might ask before they join. As much as there are general questions that you want to answer, you want to make sure to address objections as well. So before you start answering general questions, take a moment to identify the main objections that your audience would have. These should form the foundation for at least half of the questions you answer.

For example, for my program, one of the objections is "I don't have enough credibility to speak on stage and sell yet." So I should ask a question like "What if I don't have much credibility or client testimonials yet, can I still sell from stage successfully?" Of course, the answer is yes because social proof is only one aspect of successfully creating a high-converting presentation. I always recommend when people are starting out to launch their program in a pilot format, which gives the new audience a chance to experience your transformation or offer at a reduced price in exchange for a review or testimonial.

Let's say you're selling a health and fitness program and an objection is "I don't have access to a gym." So you want to ask a question like "What if I don't have access to a gym, can I still do your program successfully?"

Usually, the main objections will be around:

- **Time:** "I'm really busy right now; how can I fit this in with my current schedule?"
- **Access:** "What do I have access to, and how long do I have access for?"
- **Guarantee:** "What if the program isn't a right fit for me; can I get a refund?"
- **Support:** "What if I get stuck; how can I get help?"
- **Uniqueness:** "How is this course different from other ones on the same topic?"
- **Confidence:** "I don't feel like I'm ready yet; will this help me get more confidence quickly?"
- **Experience:** "I'm new to this industry" or "I'm already experienced in this industry; will this still help me?"

You may have noticed I didn't include money in this list, because the purpose of your presentation and your offer is to show enough value that the price is no longer the objection. If you can show the value of the transformation that your offer provides, price shouldn't be their main objection.

After you've answered some of your preprepared questions, you can go to the audience and answer any final questions they have. A great way to answer questions is to share an example or a story of someone in your program who had that same question and what their experience was. So rather than answering the question directly, you share it in a story-based answer.

Part IV

Putting Yourself Out There

Chapter 11

Get Yourself on Stage

So often I see people waiting for an opportunity to speak. I was running a workshop recently when a student came up to me and asked, "Colin, how do I get more speaking engagements?"

I remember asking him if he had declared to the world that he is a speaker. He looked a little confused. So I said to him, "Let's talk really practically. Have you put on your social media that you are a speaker? Have you put on your website that you speak and what specific topics you speak on? When people ask you, do you say that part of what you do is speaking for a living?"

I believe that the world will reflect back to you the identity you're putting forward. A big part of stepping into being a speaker is declaring to the world that you speak. Using this as the basis, which is essentially giving yourself permission, let's talk about both how to build your own stage and how to get onto other people's stages.

Build Your Own Stage

I was sitting in a workshop and for the first time hearing the presenter talk about how he had an online course that he would sell to a new group of people every month via an online webinar. He unpacked the journey of living in the city and hustling for clients daily and then making the transition to stop trying to network one-on-one for sales and start being the person on stage speaking to the group. He started running his own virtual events and webinars monthly where he would make an offer for his online course. The money he was making each month was more than I was making in six months in my business. He had left the city and moved to a coastal community where he now delivered one presentation per month, making a six-figure monthly salary and living the dream by the beach.

I was new in my entrepreneurial journey, and hearing him talk about the money he was making, the clients he was getting, and, more importantly, the lifestyle that he had, made me so excited. I came home from that workshop ecstatic and said to my wife, "I know exactly what I want to do to build the business."

Starting from Scratch

When I set out to start running my own webinars, it was really tough because I had no email database, very little social media following, and just a small list of old clients who were not necessarily the right fit for my new offers. So I set out to start running my own online events. I started to post about the fact that I was going to be hosting a high-value masterclass teaching on a specific topic. I ended up getting around 100 people registered for the event and having 60 or so people show up live. As I started hosting these regular online events, I was using them mainly as an opportunity to teach new content and grow my email database. Getting some repetitions in place gave me so much more confidence when it came to starting to run presentations to sell an offer. Over the last 16 years, I've run hundreds of online presentations and made millions of dollars. But for me, it all started with an inspiring story of someone who made the transition from hustle to leverage and lifestyle.

I think one of the fastest ways to build your business is to build your own stage (aka host your own events). There are many different types of stages out there, but essentially they are categorized into two main types: virtual stages and in-person stages. Personally, I think it's easiest to start with virtual stages—these can be webinars, virtual events, virtual meetings, or live video—any sort of experience where you're online and can reach people directly by doing a presentation. The good thing about these is that they are low cost and you can actually use them to build your audience.

Building Your Audience

So often people ask me, "Colin, should I build my audience before I start running my own events?" My answer is always the same: you build your audience by running your own events. When we run a promotion, we'll have thousands of people sign up to hear me do a 60-minute online presentation. If I had waited to have a big audience before I started running my own presentations, I wouldn't be writing this book—I would still be waiting.

I remember one of my students said to me she didn't have an online course yet and she wanted to simply sell her one-to-one coaching services. She hosted her first webinar and had about 60 people sign up, 25 people showed up live, and she sold five of her one-to-one coaching services—making more money in that one presentation to that small audience than she'd ever thought possible.

For me, one of the benefits of building your own stage is that it's your own audience. What I mean by that is you have full permission to share whatever content you like and make whatever offer you want to make. You don't need permission from any external force. Obviously, there is some work that needs to go into pulling together an audience interested in your topic, but let me tell you that it's worth the work.

Building your own audience is like going fishing in a fish farm that you've built. Imagine I said to you that you had to catch a fish for me, and I gave you a rod and reel and said you can either go fishing in the open ocean or go fishing in a fish farm. The odds of you catching a fish in the open ocean are a lot slimmer than in a fish farm. When you build your own stage and own audience, essentially you are curating an experience whereby you can find clients in a targeted small area. You don't want to be trolling the open seas of social media where people are there for all different types of purposes. Create your own fish farm and you'll have lots of clients to help.

Focusing Your Topic

Think about the fact that when someone shows up to listen to your presentation, they are intentionally coming to learn and grow. They've shown up for your specific topic and to listen to you. There's something magical and exciting about that. Rather than being there for a general purpose, they are there to learn and grow in your chosen topic. It's with that intention that when they show up, they are more likely to say yes to one of your offers in this environment than in any other.

Some insights I've learned about building your own stage are that being specific about the topic is really important. If you're hosting an online virtual event about parenting, you're going to get a lot of people who are obviously interested in parenting, but it's still a very broad topic. But if you ran a virtual event about parenting children in middle school, the parents that show up will have a hyper-sensitivity to your content.

I usually find that the more narrow you can be on the topic, the more powerful the presentation will be and the more sales it will result in, if that is your desire.

As another example, imagine you are hosting an event for photographers. This obviously has some narrowness to it, but it's also going to attract lots of different types of photographers. If you were to instead host the event specifically for luxury wedding photographers, you're going to attract your ideal customer avatar, and therefore the offer you make at the end will be so much more profitable. Essentially what I'm saying here is that to build your own stage—which is essentially to host your own event—you are better off being specific about who it's for and the topic you're covering.

Confidence and Commitment

It does take a level of confidence and decisiveness to host your own event. If you're hosting an in-person event, you obviously need to find a physical space where you would love to host it. A lot of the time, putting down a deposit on a space is a really good motivator for you to fill the event with your ideal customer avatar. The first in-person event I ever ran was focused on teaching presentation skills. I booked an office venue in a local business area for a couple hundred dollars, and I ended up having nine people register for the one-day presentation skills training. That was one of the most enjoyable workshops I'd ever run because not only did I have a great group of people, but it was my group. It was a group that had come to learn directly from me. From this group of nine people, I ended up signing four coaching clients, so the income just kept flowing from it.

If you're looking to host an in-person event, the hardest part is getting people to register. If you are just starting out,

I recommend creating a specific topic and pricing it so that it's accessible to most of your audience. The reason I say this is because once you have people in the room, that's when the magic happens.

A lot of people make the mistake of trying to make money on the initial ticket sales. This is a really hard path, as the audience is fairly cold to you at that point. However, once you get them in the room, that's when you can deliver great content, build deep rapport, and sell a premium offer.

I recently saw one of my students host her first one-and-a-half-day in-person event with 18 people showing up. She delivered great value and then made an offer. She had 8 people take up the offer and made $57,500. That's pretty cool, right? Making that amount of money with less than 20 people in the room.

That's why I say it's best to make your initial ticket price accessible to as many people as possible. Then, when they are in the room and have built trust with you, that's when you make your offer. Using this strategy, you'll make a lot more money than if you were to try to make all your money from initial ticket sales.

As I mentioned, hosting a virtual event via a webinar or online streaming platform is one of the cheapest and easiest ways to get started. As long as you've have a great topic that is narrow enough to attract a specific type of person, you should be good to get started. One pattern I've noticed is some people continually say one day they're going to host their own events. They say "someday I'll run an event" or "someday I will deliver a presentation," but the problem is that someday never comes.

One of the recommendations I give to all my students is to declare to the world that you are hosting a presentation at a specific time on a specific day and allow people to register for it. As soon as you have one person registered for your event, you have to show up. As an entrepreneur, you don't have a boss—your boss is your calendar. And the thing that's on your calendar is a presentation that clients have signed up to, and if you don't show up to it, your reputation is at stake.

If you need motivation to deliver your first presentation that you host yourself, put it out into the world and allow people to register for it. That way you can't back out of it, and it will be the motivation to get you started. Once you experience hosting your own online or in-person events, you'll be hooked.

My encouragement for you is to choose a date sometime in the future, create a topic that you would love to speak on, and share it with the world. Allow them to sign up and register, and you'll be running your own event and building your own audience in no time.

Leverage Other People's Stages

Imagine skipping all the hard work that it takes to build an audience and simply walking into a group of people that trust you and landing a whole bunch of clients from it. That is one of the incredible opportunities of leveraging other people's stages, where you speak at other people's events and community experiences. This could be hosting a webinar for one of the monthly educational talks that someone promises in their program, speaking at a breakout room at a conference, or going live in a Facebook group that has your ideal audience. Essentially, what you get to do is leverage the trust that the event leader has with their audience, and therefore rapport is built incredibly fast.

One of the advantages of using other people's stages is that you don't have to host the event. You don't have to manage all the complexities of registration, showing up, follow-up, and all the other nuances involved. Quite regularly, I get the opportunity to teach in other people's communities. Recently, I had a chance to run a training in a large membership community for female entrepreneurs. This community had thousands of people in it who were warm to my message, and it resulted in hundreds of people connecting with me and many joining our programs. The benefit was that I had very little setup or preparation to do. All I did was show up for the event and deliver my presentation, which resulted in a flurry of leads and clients.

Soft Sells and Sharp Sells

One of the main challenges with using other people's stages is that the audience is someone else's. In other words, because you haven't built the audience, you usually don't have full permission to share whatever offer or next step you would like. This is where a soft sell or a no sell presentation comes in. Usually, I like to encourage people to do a soft sell presentation where essentially you are offering something of high value—for example, it could be a worksheet, PDF, or some sort of white paper in exchange for someone's details. You could also offer a free consultation for those people who fit certain criteria. I usually find that when you're speaking on other people's stages, a soft sell is the best approach, unless of course you have permission from them explicitly that making an offer is allowed.

Most people are scared to ask an event organizer if they can make a direct offer, which I refer to as a sharp sell. I remember speaking at a youth event early on in my coaching career, and I was asked to talk on the topic of career development. I had just recently put together my first course on the topic of career development. This was someone else's audience, so I got permission from them to make the offer. During my 90-minute presentation I delivered incredible value, and at the end, I presented my offer. They were a university-age audience and therefore didn't have a huge budget, so I adjusted the price to reflect that. I remember walking out with about $3,000 in sales.

My co-presenter, who was in a different room, came out from his session, which was running at the same time, and asked me how my session went. I said it went great, we got such great feedback, and I made about $3,000. He looked at me in complete disbelief and said, "What do you mean that you made $3,000?" I told him that I'd put together a really cool offer for this specific audience and about 10 people took it. I could tell that he was dumbfounded by the fact that I just made money directly off the back end of my presentation while he walked away with a few handshakes and claps. He later became a client of mine.

Adding Value to Access Other People's Stages

The key to getting access to other people's stages is to show them how you add value to them.

There are a lot of entrepreneurs who have large communities who are looking for high-value presentations for their group on a regular basis. If you can pull together a really great presentation that delivers high value, directly reach out to them, let them know about it and the value it has added, and provide them with proof that other groups have enjoyed your presentation, they will most definitely consider you presenting to their audience.

I've also found that there are a lot of formal organizations like clubs, organizational bodies, and other nonprofit companies that are always looking for useful presentations for their members. A lot of the time they have a large group of members who are looking for personal development as part of their membership. I've spoken at many organizational bodies—for example, you could approach a learning and development national body, a human resources national body, or the national body of whatever topic you speak on and share with them your presentation topic, the outcomes it provides, and some social proof that it was received well in previous groups.

If you are a coach or a course creator, you'll have specific expertise that can add value to many people's programs. One of the best ways to approach someone as a presenter is to get referred to them by a mutual friend. For example, if I want to speak to a certain community, I will ask around and see if anyone knows that person directly. So often I've found that it's less than three degrees of separation to the person—in fact, most of the time someone I know is really good friends with them. I'll usually ask them to introduce me, and this results in leveraged trust, which ultimately leads to getting the opportunity to speak for their community.

Audience Fit Is Important

I often use other people's audiences for the purpose of building my database and honing in on the right type of clientele that would buy from me later on. The biggest thing to consider here is making sure that the audience you're choosing is a good fit. I've had many times where I've spoken and it's resulted in very few inquiries simply because the audience wasn't a right fit.

I personally believe that you're better off having a smaller, better-fit audience than a larger, wrong-fit audience. So the main thing you want to focus on is finding communities, programs, and experiences where you can deliver value, and these people are your target audience.

One of my clients helps wedding professionals grow their business using wedding shows. She has an amazing business where she reaches out to various weddings and events, and she is able to leverage the audience that the wedding event company has pulled together. She positions it as a high-value presentation, which it is, and it leads to a consistent flow of clients for her. This is such a win-win because the event organizer provides something valuable, the clients get access to an incredible service, and she gets to help more people and grow her business in the way that she wants.

Leveraging other people's stages is such a great opportunity for you to get in front of more people and transfer the trust of the leader onto you. It does have its restrictions compared to creating your own stage, but it is one of the fastest ways to create lead flow for your programs.

Chapter 12

The Virtual Presentation Machine

Hosting an online masterclass or event is one of my favorite ways to reach an audience and get a flood of clients. There are so many advantages: it's fairly easy to run, inexpensive to set up, and expansive in who it can reach; plus it means you and the participants don't have to get on a plane. This is why I always recommend starting with virtual presentations first and then moving to in-person experiences.

Scheduling Your Presentation

My first recommendation is that you choose the date you are going to be hosting your virtual presentation. There is no hard and fast rule for this, but you want to consider your audience and when they may be available.

I typically host my presentations on a Tuesday, Wednesday, or Thursday. However, I have friends who host their webinars every week on a Monday and they absolutely crush it. So it's totally up to you what works for your schedule and your audience's availability. Just remember, because you're hosting an event, you can't suit everyone, so the best thing to do is to choose a time that works for you, and that you feel works best for the majority of your people, and go with that.

The Five Phases of Your Webinar Funnel

With the scheduling of your presentation being done, you'll move through the following five phases to host a successful virtual presentation.

Warming Phase

The warming phase is where you want to start engaging with your audience at a greater level. The top marketers in the world are always in this phase—they are consistently producing highly engaging content for their audience so that whenever they decide to host a conversion experience, they'll have a flurry of prospects who trust them and will be ready to buy.

With that being the goal, I want you to consider the warming phase as being a really intentional time where you create highly engaging content and show up for your audience at a greater level. Typically, this will last for anywhere from one to six weeks prior to starting registrations.

Some things you can do at this phase:

- Send one or two emails a week that have high-quality content so that your audience starts engaging with you and you become front of mind for them.
- If you have a podcast, find your most popular topics and revisit them so that your listenership increases.
- If you're posting on social media or YouTube, produce content that has previously shown to be highly engaging but also aligns with the presentation you're about to host.
- Create simple educational videos and content where the audience finds value and builds trust with you.

If you do the warming phase well, when you transition to open up registrations, they will be more excited to attend your event and hear about your offer.

Registration Phase

The registration phase is where you're asking your audience to sign up for your event. If you're hosting a single masterclass or webinar or if you're hosting a multipart training series, you're going to have one stand-alone page where people can register using their name, email address, or phone number. As a rule of thumb, the less information you're asking from someone, the more likely they will sign up.

After hosting hundreds of webinars and having hundreds of thousands of people register, I've found that the simpler the registration page, the better. Typically, when you have a long registration page, you're asking the audience to give you more of their time to make a decision. Obviously, you always have to test what works best for your audience, but for us and the majority of my students, I've found that a shorter registration page is more effective than a long one.

In this phase, you're going to be:

- Emailing your list (who is ideally more engaged because you've warmed them up in the previous phase)
- Posting on social media
- Producing video content on YouTube
- Publishing podcasts
- Running paid advertising

All of these should point to a single registration page where you're asking people to register for the webinar. Typically, this registration phase lasts for anywhere between 7 and 14 days. Initially, when people hear that, they feel like it's a really short time—and it is. But you have to consider the attention span of people. If they register for an online event more than two weeks out, they'll typically forget about it. I recommend starting your direct invitation to your audience no more than two weeks out from the event.

If you're new to this game, I recommend choosing one or two of the promotional avenues I've listed. If you focus on too many, your time and energy will be spread too thin. Choose the platform where you have the greatest engagement and lean into that.

In this phase, you will feel like you're talking about your webinar a lot, and you'll probably find that people either unsubscribe from your emails, don't engage with your content as much, or don't watch as much of your videos. This is all very normal because the focus of this period is about getting them to decide whether they want to attend the event you're hosting. This is less about providing high value and more about giving them a desirable invitation for your event.

Typically, I recommend sending anywhere between three to six emails to your database inviting them to your event within this two-week period. Remember to create variety in the way that you promote your event—you could share a personal story, case study, helpful insights, and educational content, but remember the main call to action will be to register. Stay focused in this period, and you'll get a bunch of people signed up excited to hear from you.

Anticipation Phase

The anticipation phase starts the minute someone registers for your webinar. This phase is all about getting them excited to show up live for your presentation. With online events, you'll typically find less than 50% of people will show up live for a presentation. Depending on whether your audience is coming from organic sources or paid advertising will significantly impact the show-up rate.

If the majority of traffic is coming from an organic audience source like your email list or your social following, the show-up rate will be higher—anywhere from 25% to 60%. If you have a large portion of your audience coming from paid advertising, the show-up rate will tend to be lower—anywhere from 10% to 30%. Don't stress too much about this; just realize that the goal is to get as many people as you can to show up to the live presentation.

Here are three ways you can get them to show up excited and anticipating a great experience:

1. **Incentivize them:** Give them a reason to show up. This could be promising them an exclusive downloadable resource that only people who show up live will receive. You can also highlight the exciting content you'll be sharing and focus on results that previous attendees have achieved.

2. **Remind them:** Use calendar invitations and a series of emails or text messages highlighting when the presentation will be, based on their time zone. People get really busy, so make sure you're reminding them about your event and making it easy for them to access the link when you go live.

3. **Reframe resistances:** Address any resistances they might have after signing up. This could be conflicts with other appointments, sudden busy schedules, or nervousness about showing up live to the event.

Here's an example of addressing these resistances:

"You're registered for our masterclass coming up, but I bet you've gotten really busy since registering. You may have even had other appointments book over the top. This is really normal, but what's most important is that you decide your priority. If you are committed to the topic we'll be talking about in this live presentation, I encourage you to prioritize this over anything else you've got going on. Life will always be busy, but it's successful people who choose the right priorities in their lives that see the success others desire. Looking forward to seeing you live at the masterclass."

This is just an example—use your own words and language. The important thing is to realize that there will be resistances and objections that come up in your audience prior to showing up to your presentation. Make sure to address these as part of your anticipation email sequence leading into the live delivery.

Delivery Phase

The delivery phase is where you do your presentation. This will be you showing up live, delivering your presentation to the audience that shows up. We've spent a lot of this book focusing on crafting and creating a high-converting presentation, so this is your time to shine. Deliver incredible content that creates an immense desire for people to want to learn more and commit to themselves in your program.

If you're hosting a single webinar, this will go for anywhere between one and two hours. If you're hosting a multiday virtual experience, this could span three to five days. It doesn't matter so much how long the presentation is but rather that you show up as the best version of yourself.

On the day of delivery:

- Make sure to remind the audience that you will be showing up live.
- Give them special bonuses for attending live.
- Test your equipment at least 24 hours before you go live to avoid any glitches.
- You'll deliver your presentation and then make your offer. That offer could be:
  - A sharp sell that leads directly into joining your program
  - A soft sell that invites them to download something valuable or book a call with you or your team
  - A no sell that asks for feedback on your content and follows up with them later

If you are hosting your own webinar, I typically recommend at least a sharp or soft sell, depending on the program you want to offer your audience. When I first started out, I did deliver some no-sell presentations—these were great for building my confidence, and if you want to start there, you totally can. However, I've found that for many of my students, at least starting with a soft sell is very comfortable as the first step.

Follow-up Phase

After you've delivered your live presentation, you're going to have two groups of people: those who showed up live and heard your presentation and offer and those who missed it. I recommend segmenting these two groups because the people who showed up live will have context for the follow-up sequence you're about to share with them. If someone didn't attend your event, what you're about to send them could feel like it's come out of the blue.

Let's keep this really simple. I recommend sending the first two emails separately to each of these two groups:

For those who attended live:

- Send follow-up communication thanking them for attending.
- Talk about the great feedback received.
- Transition directly into the next step (joining a program or booking a call).

For those who didn't attend:

- Send an email saying you're sorry to miss them.
- Provide a limited-time replay (available for three to seven days).
- In the second email, remind them of the replay and discuss the next step offer.

After these first two emails, which are typically sent in the first 24 hours after the event, you can synchronize both groups and start sending the same communications to each. Remember, the main focus of this phase is to get them to decide whether they want to take the next step. A mistake that many people make is getting distracted by trying to provide more educational content in this phase. If you do that, it'll simply distract your audience from making a decision.

Here's a daily communication sequence you could use over a seven-day follow-up period:

1. Share your excitement about your program and the benefits and results you've seen.

2. Share a case study story of a previous student and their results.

3. Address frequently asked questions or typical objections.

4. Focus on a personal story that connects with your customer avatar.

5. Share social proof and client examples.

6. Add a special bonus that wasn't announced in the presentation.

7. Focus on the deadline and enrollment period closing.

If you follow this flow, it will build trust in your offer, resonance with your audience, and urgency in their decision. You always want to make sure you have a finish date—if you don't have a really clear day when enrollment closes, your conversion will be half of what it could be.

Putting It All Together

In review, a successful webinar funnel consists of five key phases that work together to create an effective virtual presentation system. It begins with the warming phase, where you engage your audience through consistent, valuable content across various platforms. This is followed by the registration phase, where you focus on getting sign-ups through a simple, streamlined process over a 7–14 day period. The anticipation phase then kicks in, working to maximize live attendance through incentives, reminders, and addressing potential objections. The delivery phase is where you present your content and make your offer, whether it's a sharp sell, soft sell, or no sell. Finally, the follow-up phase involves segmenting your audience between those who attended live and those who didn't, providing tailored communication to each group and maintaining momentum toward a decision.

Once you've delivered this system a few times, you'll get into a rhythm whereby you or your team can run this same play over and over again. I've seen students go through a really fast learning curve in the initial 90 days, and then the whole process becomes mostly automated. The exciting thing is that you can reuse and repurpose the content you've created in the five phases I've just outlined. That means that each time you do this, it becomes easier and easier, and the results get better and better.

Resource: I've created a useful webinar promotional map that visually shows where you should do your emails, posts, and communication prior and after the webinar. Simply go to www.onepresentationawaybook.com/resources.

Case Study Breakout: Local Buffalo Mom Makes $40,000 Per Month with One Presentation

Lindsay Van Harssel is an amazing mom and online course creator from Buffalo, New York, who helps wedding professionals fill their calendars with hot leads that turn into raving clients with wedding shows. When Lindsay first joined our Sell

From Stage programs, she had a really strong desire to build a leveraged online course business but had been struggling for years to make that a reality. On top of this, Lindsay shared with me that she has a beautiful young son with a disability. She wasn't willing to compromise being there for him as a priority, but her predicament was that her business growth was slow and required a lot of her time and effort.

She ended up building one presentation that she delivers to her ideal audience once a week. She told me that the setup for this presentation takes very little time because it's the same presentation she delivers every time. She's initially partnered with wedding show organizers, and she becomes an add-on experience that is a part of wedding events across the United States. This strategy gave her some initial momentum, and now she also uses paid ads to grow her weekly webinar. She's able to get in front of her ideal clients and gets an incredible conversion rate. She's grown her business from just a few thousand dollars a month to more than $40,000 a month consistently, delivering one presentation per week and working only a few hours. With every presentation, she is also growing her email list by 500 people per week, so the trickle-on effect keeps going as those people end up buying other programs that her business offers.

But the best part is that not only does she have more resources to look after her family and her son, but she has freedom. She has freedom to be there at those special moments when her son needs her and the space in her schedule to show up for her family in the way she's always desired.

Every time I hear Lindsay's story, it makes me emotional because it reminds me of the reason why I do what I do: to help entrepreneurs just like her create a leveraged sales system that gives them the money, freedom, and fulfillment they have always dreamed of.

Chapter 13

Attracting an Audience

I remember a phone call I received from one of my clients who had just delivered his first large conference presentation. Previously, he had spoken to audiences of 100 or so, but this was his first big one—a 5,000-person auditorium at a main industry event in the United States. Heading into the presentation, he was incredibly nervous, but as the true entrepreneur he is, he had put in the time and effort to practice his presentation and refine it to a point where it became part of him, not just a presentation he was giving. He spoke for 45 minutes, delivered some incredible stories, and ended with a standing ovation. He called me right after he stepped off the stage and said, "Colin, I've built a lot of companies and made a lot of money in my life, but that was the most exhilarating experience I've ever had. I feel like I'm born to do this." The cool thing was that the event organizer had tapped him on the shoulder and said, "I want you to be the main headline speaker for next year's conference."

Speaking in front of an engaged audience, whether in person or virtual, is one of the most euphoric experiences you can have. The thrill of seeing people laughing and leaning in or commenting enthusiastically in the chat is such a blast. That's why I wanted to share with you how to attract an audience. The truth is, you can have the greatest presentation and the most incredible offer, but if no one is there to hear it, there will be no point to it. This chapter is about filling your events with excited, committed people.

Let's discuss the different ways that you can attract your own audience so that once you step on the stage, you have people to win over. The question is, how do you create a stadium of people who are excited to hear from you and watch your magic unfold? Let's explore some of my favourite ways to generate traffic for virtual and in person events. They're essentially categorized into three main areas: your own traffic, affiliate traffic, and paid traffic.

Your Own Traffic

Your own traffic can be achieved through a variety of avenues; this chapter will include my favorite ways including organic social media, email lists, podcasts, and YouTube.

Organic Social Media

Your social media is such a crucial part of being successful as a personal brand. I remember when social media was in its growth phases. I was very laissez-faire with it—I enjoyed it but was mainly just posting pictures of my latest cappuccino. I remember a conversation with my wife when she challenged me to take my online branding presence to the next level. We started working together on a personal brand strategy whereby organic social media growth was one of the main goals. Organic social media is content you post manually (or scheduled) on your social platform as opposed to using a paid media to spread it for you. Your organic social media will mainly go out to your followers with some extra reach to nonfollowers depending on the social algorithm.

One of the keys to my success was that I partnered with the right people in the areas that weren't my absolute genius. I was lucky enough that my wife is a genius in the area of building social media following. Here are some of the secrets that took me from several hundred to tens of thousands of followers on social media and have helped me to generate millions of dollars in revenue.

First, I recommend focusing on a social media platform where your audience is. For some people this will be Facebook; for others it will be Instagram, LinkedIn, X, etc. There are constantly new social media platforms popping up, so you need to be aware of where your audience is so that you can reach them effectively.

Another important element in choosing your social media platform is thinking about how much you enjoy the platform. Especially in the beginning stages, you're going to be posting a lot of your own content, and if you enjoy the platform, you'll tend to spend more time on it. But the key thing to remember here is that you can't be a consumer of the content—you must be a creator. Amateurs jump on social media and consume content for their own enjoyment; from a social media perspective, consumers are the product that social media is selling. But as soon as you become a creator on social media, the equation changes, and you can use it extremely effectively to grow your reach and your revenue.

One of the most important things to do is to have consistency in your posting and study what is working on your platform of choice. Social media is continually changing, and what works one month won't work the next. I like to follow social media accounts that teach useful social growth content so that I can replicate what's working in the marketplace using my own personal style.

Attracting an Audience

To build a following on social media, you must understand how to post engaging content. One of my favorite ways of doing this is starting with a really good hook, which is essentially the first three seconds of a video or the first sentence of a social media post. An example of a hook is "The five things you must never do on a sales webinar." That hook speaks about avoiding pain, but it also creates a sense of curiosity. It makes the reader want to read on and leads to content that would be relevant around that topic.

Another example of a hook is "How to sell on webinars without feeling like you're selling." This one speaks about a desire that the audience has and also addresses something they want to avoid. Essentially, it's saying get this pleasurable experience without this unpleasurable effect.

Studying people who have big followings, you'll notice that they are very good at hooks. From my experience, 80% of a good social media post is about starting with a good hook. Make the hook relevant to your target audience and aligned with the event you're promoting, and you'll get a lot of interest and registrations for your online and in-person events.

Email Lists

Your money is in your email list. For me, the most important asset of my entire business is my email list. The reason it's so important is because I have full control over it. I'm not at the beck and call of social media platforms and how they decide the algorithm should act on that given day.

There's discussion out there that email is dead or that email isn't what it used to be. Sure, it's going to change over the next years; however, my experience has been that it is currently still the most powerful way to invite people to your presentations, share powerful content that builds trust, and ultimately generate clients.

When I first started out, I remember using a spreadsheet where I tracked people's names and my emails to them. That my friend, is a very clunky and poor way to manage your email list. I don't recommend you do this—but this was back in the days of the Wild Wild West when I had no clue what I was doing. There are extremely powerful and cost-effective email management software applications you can use now that will build, send, and track everything. Make sure to use software that gives you the power to connect with your database in an effective, efficient, and safe way.

I used to get quite upset when people unsubscribed from my emails. Now I have tens of thousands of people who read my emails every single week, and it doesn't bother me if they unsubscribe. For me, if someone unsubscribes, they probably weren't a right fit for what I do, and I totally respect that. I've had people sit on my email list for years, opening almost every email I send and not purchasing anything. Then all of a sudden, they buy something really significant from me and my business. You'll have some people who enter your email list who want to buy right away, and then you'll have others who take their time. As a generalization, my experience has been that when someone first gets on your email list, they are more inclined to want to do business with you than if they are on your email list for years.

A lot of students ask me whether they should build their email list with a freebie or some sort of guide before they launch their first presentation, but I always recommend that you don't need a big email list to start out. In fact, your webinar registration form will build your email list with people who are interested in your topic and ready to buy.

I recommend you email your list at least once a week—for some people it's more than that, but at a minimum, you should be sending something valuable every single week. Here's a bit of a formula I use for a weekly email. First, you want to hook them with a great subject line. You could write the most incredible email on earth, but if someone doesn't open your email, it's useless. Just as in social media, where the first sentence at the top of your social media post is worth 80% of the whole post, the quality of your subject line is even more important.

AI has made it incredibly easy to write great hooks. You can go to almost any AI platform and ask it to write a hook for a topic that you're writing on for a specific target market. In fact, you could even copy and paste your entire email and ask it to come up with 10 different hooks that would be great as email subject lines.

Once you've got people to open your email, the next thing you'll want to do is engage them with some sort of problem or desire. This could be a really good question or a powerful statement that speaks to their pain or pleasure. For example, I could ask the question, "Have you ever struggled to find the right story to tell in your presentations?" That question is a universal yes for most people—they resonate with the idea, and they're interested in telling better stories.

Once you've reestablished some curiosity in the email, you're going to want to amplify the impact of getting this right or getting it wrong. From there, you can share a personal story or a case study of someone who's got an incredible result, and then you can link it directly to some sort of call to action. This could be for them to sign up to a presentation that you have coming up or to click some sort of link to watch a video. Just make sure the action you ask them to do aligns with the content you've been discussing in the email.

If you do this right, you should have a good click-through rate, and it will result in a flow of registrations for your presentations.

Note I've created a vault of some of my best emails that you can model for promoting your presentations or engaging your email list. Simply go to www.onepresentationawaybook .com/resources.

Podcasts

Podcasts are one of my favorite consumable platforms. My experience has been that podcasting is one of the platforms that accelerates trust the fastest. There have been two occasions where I have listened to a podcast for several months and gradually built trust and appreciation for a content creator, and this has directly led to me signing up to one of their high-level mastermind programs, where I invested a significant amount of money.

There's something about being in someone's ears while they are walking around their streets in the morning, running on the treadmill, or driving their car. You become part of their life, and the level of trust that's built is incredible. For me, a podcast is very much a trust-building platform as opposed to an audience-growth platform. What I mean by that is my podcast, *Expert Edge Podcast*, is less about growing a massive audience and more about building loyal listeners.

For me, podcasts have a very long tail: they last a long time, but they also take a while to grow. Where social media platforms can be a place that you can go viral quickly, podcasts are usually a slow burn that you must stay consistent on over time. At the time of writing this, I've been running my podcast for more than five years, and it is still one of my favorite places for creating new content and sharing it with the world.

One of the challenges I find with podcasts is that it's difficult to get feedback and responses. Where in a presentation you can instantly know if the audience is resonating with it based on their response, in a podcast it is more difficult to find that out. Other than asking your audience formally to give you feedback or getting the occasional review, you really don't know how much impact your podcast is making. The interesting thing is that whenever I go to industry events, the thing that people stop me for and say they love is my podcast. I think the reason for this is because you spend so much time in people's lives and because it's long-form content, it genuinely creates an emotional resonance with them. Building your own podcast is a fantastic platform for creating an extremely loyal and engaged following, and it can also be used very effectively for inviting your loyal and warm listeners to one of your presentations where they can decide if they would like to work with you.

For me, podcasts also bleed into affiliate traffic, which I'll talk about later in this chapter. Being a guest on other people's podcasts is one of my favorite ways to expand my reach and influence. The cool thing about guesting on other people's podcasts is that you're engaging with their loyal following. Podcast listeners are people who love to learn — they're happy to spend 30 to 60 minutes or more just listening and learning about a topic.

So if you get the chance to be a guest on someone else's podcast, do it. As much as I get requests in my inbox to be on people's podcasts, I also ask to be a guest on podcasts. Sometimes I'll email the host directly, message them on social media, or ask to be referred through a mutual friend. Don't be afraid to ask to be on someone's podcast—most podcasters are looking for people with high-quality content all the time.

Send them some examples of different podcasts you've been on previously and pitch them a specific topic and how this would benefit their audience. Most of the time you'll have people say no. Don't take it personally; all you need is a few yeses and you'll gain some momentum. Using the power of podcasts and being guests on other people's podcasts will not only expand your reach, but you'll have a lot of fun. And you'll build a great relationship with the host, which can lead to other collaborations and work together in the future.

Here is a pro tip: one of the best ways to get on other people's podcasts is to invite them on yours. When you lead with generosity first, most of the time they will reciprocate and ask if they can have you on their podcast in return. This, for me, is one of the best ways of asking without asking. Find some people you look up to, invite them to be on your podcast, and eventually it'll lead to you being on theirs.

YouTube

YouTube is one of the most incredible search engines out there. Most people misunderstand what YouTube is—they think it's a social platform, but it's not; it's a search engine. YouTube is essentially Google for videos. Building your YouTube channel is another fantastic way of building trust with your audience fast. I love YouTube because you can be hyper-specific with the topics you focus on, and when people search for it, you can show up in their results.

To build a following, first of all, you must be consistent. Posting a weekly video around a specific topic is recommended. As usual, your hook is really important to start with—in fact, it's usually the first thing you create for the video. The interesting thing about YouTube is that the image thumbnail can be the difference between hundreds and tens of thousands of views. Following channels that are up-to-date with best practices is one of the secrets to staying current with what's working right now. Top YouTube channels will test 5 to 10 different image thumbnails for their videos to see which one performs the best before they settle on the right one to keep.

I also love YouTube because essentially it's a video presentation platform. You get the chance to present your ideas in a format where people can hear you, see you, and ultimately feel your presence. Think about YouTube as the "how-to" platform. Most people go to YouTube because they have a problem they want to solve, and if you can show them how to solve it through powerful video content, trust will be built very quickly, and they'll end up either subscribing to your email list or becoming customers right away.

We use YouTube to amplify the speed at which trust is developed with a new audience member. In our initial email sequences, we'll point them to certain videos that I know resonate with my ideal customer avatar.

Affiliate Traffic

Affiliate traffic is essentially leveraging other people's audiences for the purpose of expanding your reach and gaining more registrations for your presentations. All of the platforms I mentioned in the "Your Own Traffic" section—including social media, email, podcasts, and YouTube—can be used as an affiliate traffic platform. For example, you can go live on social media and collaborate with a friend, you can get included in someone's email newsletter promoting your events, you can get on someone else's podcast, and you can be featured on their YouTube channel. I've used all of these methods in my business to grow my audience and reach.

Incentivizing Affiliates

An affiliate is essentially having someone else promote your event, webinar, or in-person seminar to their audience in exchange for a share of revenue. Affiliates have been one of my favorite ways of growing our business. When I first launched my flagship program Sell From Stage Academy®, I was running a webinar every month and each time partnering with a new affiliate who would promote it to their list.

Essentially, how this works is I would reach out to someone I knew had an audience that would like and most probably join my program. I would discuss with them some of the results that I've got previously in our promotions and then share with them how much they could earn per person that joined the program.

Affiliate commissions range significantly depending on industry and product. But as a guide, I recommend being more generous with your affiliate commission because it incentivizes the affiliate dramatically to promote your program. Typically in the expert industry, you'll see anywhere between 30% and 50% affiliate commissions paid on a digital product. If you're talking about higher-ticket group coaching and mastermind programs, the affiliate commission typically ranges between 10% and 30%. Obviously, this is a guide, and you have to decide what works for you, but I recommend being generous with your affiliate commission.

One way to think about it is to realize that you wouldn't get the sale without the affiliate. Because they have provided the lead source, that person probably would not have joined your program if they had not promoted it to their audience. Sometimes people think that it's crazy to give away 50% of your top-line revenue to an affiliate, but to me it makes sense because you wouldn't have the sale otherwise. As long as the profit margin on your program is there to support a strong affiliate program, this is one of my favorite ways to grow.

Some of the other advantages of using affiliates is that your list will grow with people who have a faster trajectory of trust building with you because you have been referred by someone they already trust. Think of it like a referral program on steroids. I know when someone refers me to someone else, I'm a lot more open to working with them compared to someone who I found randomly online. The same goes for having affiliates who promote you—you'll get the trust transfer from them to you.

The Affiliate Alignment Formula

There are three questions I ask myself to work out if an affiliate is a good fit. I call this the Affiliate Alignment Formula:

1. Is the audience of the affiliate a good fit for my program? For me, this is the most important element to consider when choosing affiliates. I usually take into consideration my ideal customer avatar and then look at the types of programs they are promoting and their typical audience, and it's fairly easy to work out if they're going to be a good fit. The audience fit will range from being absolutely the wrong fit to being completely the right fit.

2. How engaged is their audience? There are many people out there who rarely engage with their audience—they don't post on social media or send regular emails. The more engaged the person is with their audience, the better an affiliate they will be.

3. How big is their audience? Notice that this is actually the last question I ask because for me, what's more important is that their audience is the right fit for my program

and they are engaged with their audience. I've found that just because someone has a big audience doesn't mean it's going to be a successful affiliate relationship.

Figure 13.1 shows a visual representation of the three questions you should ask when choosing the right type of affiliate and how these interact.

Obviously, the goal is to ultimately find and partner with affiliates who have a big audience that is highly engaged and is the right fit for your programs. That is an affiliate dream partner; it's going to be rare to start with an affiliate who has all three areas dialed in. So I recommend you just start with people who have smaller audiences, or even your current students can be a great affiliates for you. As I mentioned, what's most important is ensuring that the audience is a right fit and engaged with that person's content.

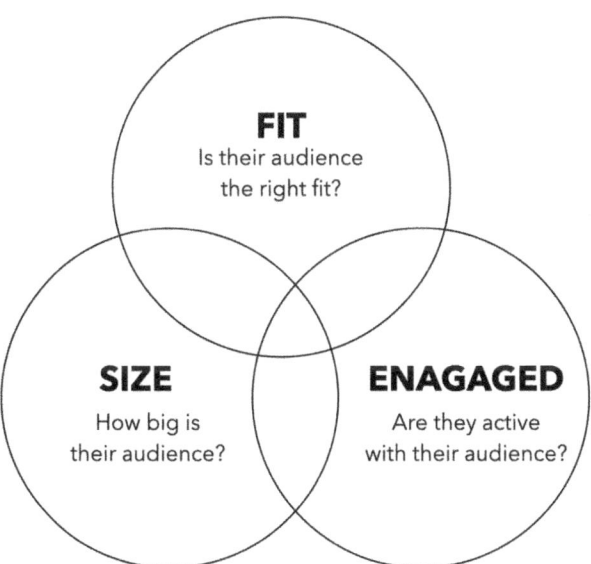

Figure 13.1 Showing the Affiliate Alignment Formula

Attracting an Audience

Building Affiliate Relationships

Sometimes people get stuck trying to work out where on Earth they're going to find these affiliates. Let me make this really simple for you: you're going to find your affiliates in your own communities. For me, all of my best affiliates have come from within programs that I'm currently participating in as a member, from students within my own programs, or from relationships I have with someone within the industry who is happy to refer me to others.

The key with affiliates is to build some relationship first. My best affiliates have come from podcast guests, participants of a program that I'm a member of, and just friends I've made in the industry. A really simple thing to do is to look at the participants who are involved in a program that you're already doing, find someone who you think would be a good affiliate for your program, and reach out to them directly.

Mention you are a member with them in the current community and have a simple online catchup. Don't pitch them directly on your affiliate program right away—just build a relationship, and usually by the end of your conversation, it will come to asking them how you can help them grow their community. Typically they will reciprocate and ask how they can help you. You can always discuss affiliating for each other, which is one of my favorite things to do. You affiliate for them, they affiliate for you, and everyone wins.

Paid Traffic

Now let's explore probably the most advanced way of marketing, which is using paid traffic. I usually don't recommend paid traffic right from the start. For me personally, paid traffic comes in after you have tested your presentation and offer and made a few sales. Paid traffic is great for accelerating the results based on a proven conversion mechanism, like a presentation that is already converting.

However, I do believe that people generally take too long to start using paid ads. I know that was the case for me. I waited way too long to take advantage of paid ads, and I know I would have grown a lot more if I had started earlier. I recommend doing two or three presentations to test your offer and get some great feedback from your audience; then once you have a bit of evidence showing that your audience is willing to buy your program, you can take the next step: paid ads.

As you get to the higher levels of the industry, you'll quickly find out that it's very normal for people to get between 60% and 80% of their leads through paid traffic. I have friends who run multimillion-dollar businesses and use paid ads to gain 80% or more of their lead traffic. The good thing about this is that paid ads don't rely on you manually posting—they automatically put your advertising in front of your audience, and with the way AI and various algorithms are being integrated within the ads platforms, the speed at which it allows you to find your best customers is incredible.

Choosing Your Paid Ads Platform

Choosing your paid ads platform is going to be a completely unique decision for you. You must consider where your audience is and where you already have some credibility. There are many different mediums you can use paid ads to advertise your webinars and events. These can range from (but are not limited to) Facebook, Instagram, LinkedIn, YouTube, Google Ads,

TikTok, and X, and then also move into sponsorship of events. For me personally, and for most of our students, Facebook, Instagram, LinkedIn, and YouTube are my favorite mediums. That definitely has something to do with the fact that my audience is on those platforms, but also the ad managers on those platforms are highly effective.

Allocating Your Resources

One of the famous pioneers of marketing, John Wanamaker, said, "Half the money I spend on advertising is wasted; the trouble is I don't know which half." This no longer needs to be the case for you. With the digital capability and tracking that is available online now, you can see with fairly high accuracy how much it is costing you to gain a lead (which is referred to as cost per lead or CPL), and you can see how much it's costing you to gain a customer (which is referred to as cost per customer [CPC]). There are so many great metrics you can track with a high degree of accuracy from using paid traffic on social media and search-based platforms that it allows you to scale up fairly quickly.

When I first started using paid traffic, I was so freaked out. I remember having sleepless nights spending $500 to $1,000 on advertising for a webinar that I was running in the coming weeks. Now if we're running a promotion, I wouldn't even bother hosting a webinar if I was spending only a few thousand dollars. I'll invest significantly in paid traffic for any of our larger promotions. For me, learning to feel comfortable spending more and more money on paid advertising is like climbing a big mountain. A few of my friends have climbed parts of Everest, and they talk about the fact that at each camp you have to acclimatize; that's essentially what I recommend with paid advertising. Start small and gradually you'll feel more comfortable allocating a higher budget to paid ads.

You don't have to be an expert on the ads platform that you choose either. I always recommend working with a professional who understands how to deliver ads effectively on the platform you choose. Learning how to use the various ads platforms can be a full-time job. Fairly quickly when I started, I realized spending my time trying to work out where to place my pixel wasn't the best use of my time. So I always recommend allocating some of your budget to hiring an ads professional who can do the technical work for you.

The one thing I don't recommend outsourcing is the ads creation itself. That is something you really should be spending time on to understand and master. I'll explain a simple ads formula that has seen great success for us and our students in the next section.

Creating Paid Ads

There is an effective formula for creating paid ads, and it all comes down to your hook, copy, call to action, and your visuals.

First, you want to come up with a really good hook. That hook has to create curiosity combined with desire or pain for your target audience. For example, if I was wanting to host a webinar teaching moms how to homestead, I could use a hook like "Here is the one homesteading habit that made growing my garden easy." Can you see that this type of hook creates curiosity and desire? You could even turn it into a question like "Are you ready to make homesteading easy for you and your family?"

Second, after you do the hook, you want to create some engaging copy. This is going to connect with the audience's pain or pleasure based on the hook itself. Following this example, I could say something like:

"Homesteading can be incredibly frustrating. It seems to take all your time and you end up with one or two edible vegetables that won't even feed your two-year-old. It doesn't have to be this way. In fact, I've discovered over the last seven years of homesteading that creating a Sustainable Homesteading Schedule is the secret to having success in this area. When you create a Sustainable Homesteading Schedule, you will no longer need lots of discipline or hard work—you will just simply follow the process and the results will flourish from there."

Third, you'll invite the reader of the advertisement to take an action. This could be to register for your upcoming webinar. You could say something like:

"This is the very reason I'm hosting the Homesteading Made Easy Masterclass. It will be a step-by-step workshop for moms who are ready to live a homesteading lifestyle and provide organic, fulfilling, and enriching food for them and their family. Click on the link below and register right now."

The final piece of most ads will be some sort of image or video to go along with it. You need to test lots of different types of images or videos to see what works best. These could be as simple as a photo of you with the hook that you are using in the advertising on the image. If you're using a video, you could pretty much just read the script that is in the written advertising. As long as it has a great hook, connects with their pain or their pleasures, and gives them a call to action, that will take you a long way.

Building Your Audience Through Persistence

The simple formula of having a hook, engaging with their pain or pleasures, and then inviting them to take an action is a great structure to follow when you're designing paid advertising. The interesting thing is that after running thousands of ads, sometimes the ones that you think are going to do great end up flopping, and the ones that you wrote off at the start end up being your best advertising.

Professional marketers understand that following a formula increases the chances of success, but ultimately the market decides what they like. Don't take it personally if you feel like you've created the best advertising and it doesn't work—just keep trying different variations and eventually the market will tell you which advertising they love.

The great thing is that once you've created a few really good ads, you can reuse these ads many times. Personally, I've had ads that we used consistently over 12 to 15 months and they still work every single day. Paid advertising will put butane on the fire that's already burning in your business and take you from growing to scaling quickly.

Note that I've compiled a swipe file of some of our most successful advertisings that you can model in your next paid ads campaign to fill your events: Simply go to www.onepresen tationawaybook.com/resources.

Building an audience to attend your presentations involves three main traffic sources: your own, affiliate, and paid. Your own traffic comes from the organic following you've built on platforms like social media, email lists, podcasts, and YouTube channels. These are a great place to start inviting people to events because these people already know and trust you. Affiliate traffic leverages other people's audiences through collaborations, guest appearances, and affiliate partnerships, allowing you to tap into established communities and benefit from trust transfer. Paid traffic, particularly through advertising platforms like Facebook, Instagram, LinkedIn, and YouTube, can rapidly scale your reach once you've proven your presentation and offer convert well. While each channel has its unique advantages, the key is to start with what feels manageable and gradually expand your reach across multiple platforms as your business grows.

Chapter 14

I Believe in You

As I tumble-turned to do my next lap, I swam down the 50-meter pool as the evening was starting to settle into a warm low glow. I made my strokes down the lane, and I looked through my goggles and saw my dad sitting in the stands. A few times a week, he would take me to the swimming pool where he would watch me train. As I hopped out of the pool and felt the cool breeze hit my skin, my dad came over and threw a warm towel over me and gave me my drink bottle. We sat down in the stands and talked about how I was swimming. He said to me, "Colin, you are such a great swimmer; I genuinely think you could go all the way to the Olympics. I really believe in you."

The same would happen in my baseball games. I would get up to bat and make a hit and get on base, and at the end of the game, I would walk back to the car with my dad and he would say, "Gosh, you're good at baseball, mate. If you keep going like this, I genuinely think you're going to play in the major leagues." The reality is that I didn't make it to the Olympics, and I didn't make it to the major leagues. But in terms of my industry and what I do, I feel like I could not have achieved the success I've had without having my dad believing in me. Having my dad believe in me has been a continual comfort as I've taken courageous steps to play in the major leagues of the coaching industry.

I am not naive enough to believe that many people, maybe including you, didn't have someone in your life who spoke the words "I believe in you" as you were growing up and forming who you were. So if I could be so bold as to say it, I would love to be that person for you. I want you to know that "I believe in you." I want to speak that over your life and into your heart right now. I believe in your ability to overcome adversity and make it a powerful part of your message. I believe in your ability to have the courage to stand on a stage and share your truth. I believe in your ability to feel the fear but act on the faith that you know in your heart.

The thing I didn't mention in my story is that my dad never knew his dad. He never had a dad who would take him to the swimming pool, who would watch him play baseball, or who would just hang out with him down at the park. It's incredible to think that someone who never had that in their life was able to give it as a gift to someone else. I think that as humans it's amazing how we can use our adversity and difficulty to be the catalyst for seeing change in the world.

On this journey, we have explored how you can find your ideal audience, create an irresistible offer, and share it using one high-converting signature presentation. You've discovered that you need only one presentation to see a breakthrough in your business. I want to encourage you that you are closer to your breakthrough than you even realize. Use this book as a practical guide and inspirational material to go out and serve your audience like never before, becoming a true market leader in your industry and making a real difference.

When I'm 90 years old, sitting on my rocking chair reflecting on my life, my biggest fear is not that I made some mistakes. My biggest fear is that I didn't fully go after my full potential. As much as I feel the fear of being judged, disliked, or ridiculed, my biggest fear is that at the end of my life, I would look back and feel like I didn't fully live my life.

Stepping onto the stage is one of the most invigorating, exciting, and courageous things you can do. If you feel a message in your heart and a burning desire to help people achieve more, then it is not only something you should do—I believe it is something you must do. Because if you don't, you'll be sitting on your rocking chair feeling the weight of regret instead of the joy of possibility.

You are called to the stage—not just for your own purposes, but for the purpose of spreading your message, serving your audience, and fulfilling the potential that is in your life.

I welcome you to the stage.

Acknowledgments

This book is the culmination of a 16-year journey—so far—of building my business. It's true that great businesses are never built by one person. It takes the input, guidance, and encouragement of many people to create something significant.

First, I want to acknowledge my wife, Sarah, the secret weapon I was lucky enough to partner with on this entrepreneurial journey. You are my best friend, my hero, and the greatest gift God ever gave me; I love you. To my incredible kids, Jonah and Georgia, you are the best kids I could have ever hoped for, and I'm grateful that I get to be your dad.

To the team at Wiley, thank you for the opportunity to partner with such a reputable brand and for helping to get this message into people's hands around the world. To Kelly for editing and guiding this book into its finished version, your direction and feedback were invaluable. To Shannon for taking a chance with me with this book and Leah for making the process so smooth, thank you.

To James Wedmore, who unlocked a bigger way of thinking in me and showed me what was possible beyond my current experience—thank you. To Jon Acompora, who has become a true brother in this journey—you are the epitome of a true friend, and I am forever grateful.

To my team members, who work tirelessly to support our clients, grow this message, and impact lives—thank you.

I genuinely couldn't do this without your dedication and care. To Amy Porterfield, who has inspired me to go bigger while never compromising on quality—you are a gift to this industry.

To my thousands of clients who have joined my programs and given me the privilege of being part of their journey to the next level—thank you. I don't take it for granted.

To my peer mastermind group, who have become more than business associates, but true friends, your support means the world to me. Finally, to God, who took a young boy with little direction and guided me on this journey so that I now get to help people around the world doing what I love most.

And, of course, to you the reader. You are the reason I wrote this book and the reason I push myself every day to grow. Thank you for being a part of my journey.

Much love,
Colin

About the Author

Colin is the go-to authority when you want your virtual and live presentations to get clients, not just claps. He advises the biggest names in the industry to speak and sell from both virtual and live stages, as well as more than 10,000 other entrepreneurs worldwide. Colin is a Certified Speaking Professional, who has been on the professional speaking circuit for more than a decade. He's best known for his signature program called Sell From Stage Academy®, which helps people turn every presentation into a money-making machine. He lives in Newport Beach, California with his wife and two children.

Website: https://colinboyd.co/

Social Instagram: https://www.instagram.com/colinboyd/

Facebook: https://www.facebook.com/colinboydglobal/

LinkedIn: https://www.linkedin.com/in/colinboyd/

YouTube: https://www.youtube.com/@colinboydcoaching

Next Steps

Get the *One Presentation Away* Free Resources

Get access to the downloadable templates, emails, and scripts that are a companion resource with this book.

Simply go to www.onepresentationawaybook.com/resources.

Develop Your Own Conversion Story

If you're ready to design and share a conversion story that instantly connects with your audience and attracts them toward your offers, then the conversion story formula program is a great next step.

Simply go to www.conversionstoryformula.com.

Get Access to Sell From Stage Academy® Curriculum

If you feel a calling to speak and sell from a stage, then Sell From Stage Academy® is the implementation program that couples beautifully with this book. Inside this program, taken by thousands of other entrepreneurs, you'll discover many more strategies and proven tools for building a high-converting talk that gets you clients every time you speak.

Simply go to www.sellfromstageacademy.com.

Index

Page numbers followed by *f* refer to figures.

embodying, 40–41
free, 35
and offers, 56, 94
pacing of, 146
in podcasts, 183–184
resonating with, 91–92
in signature talks, 108–111
in social media, 178–180
in stage-building, 155
summarizing, 144
topic-focused, 156–157
video, 167, 186
for virtual events, 18–19
in webinars, 136, 166–174
in workshops, 98
Content creation, 9, 54, 86, 94, 108, 183
Conversion rates:
bonuses for, 66
case study of, 115–116
definition of, 21
engagement for, 21
of live events, 24, 95
of one-to-one selling, 22
on online marketing, 23
timing for, 74
in virtual events, 18
Conversion stories, 51, 72, 107, 133, 136. *See also* Storytelling
Conversion Story Formula, 49, 72

Core premises, 43–51
examples of, 50–51
four vehicles of, 45–49
identity-based, 51
and presentation closings, 115
and results, 49–50
as single sentence, 44–45
skill-based, 50
and stories, 107, 133, 135
thing-based, 50
unique vehicle-based, 51
Cost per customer (CPC), 192
Cost per lead (CPL), 192
Covey, Stephen, 56
Customer avatars, 8, 84–85, 157, 173, 186, 188

Deadline scarcity, 74
Decision-based content, 117–119
Delivery phase of webinar funnel, 170–171, 174
Demographics, 78–79, 85
Desire-based bonuses, 65
Desire enticement, 123–127

Email databases, 154
Email lists, 180–183, 186
Email marketing. *See also* Social media

213

Index

connecting through, 14–15

delivery phase of, 170–171

ease of, 158

follow-up phase of, 172–173

hosting, 94

magic of, 23–24

as meeting format, 20–21

registration phase of, 167–168

scheduling, 165

topics for, 156

traffic for, 177–178

warming phase of, 166–167

webinar funnels in, 166–173

webinars as, 17–18

Virtual stages, 17–21, 155

Virtual summits, 19

Vulnerability, xx, 28, 39

Walker, Megan, 122

Walls of commitment, 57

Wanamaker, John, 192

Warming phase of webinar funnel, 166–167, 173

Webinars:

affiliates in, 187

certainty in, 60

conversion rates for, 115–116

developing, 135–137

ease of, 158

meeting formats vs., 20–21

in national bodies, 159

paid ads in, 175, 191–194

registration for, 181

sharp selling in, 93–94

signature talks as, 86

as virtual stages, 17, 113–155

as workshops, 97–98

Webinar funnels, 166–174

Wedmore, James, 48, 58, 100

Whales, xxi–xxii

Working guarantees, 67

Workshops. *See also* Masterclasses

of breakout speakers, 96–97

in-person, 16, 94

and masterclasses, 97–98

mastermind, 91–92

as signature talks, 103

virtual, 65

X, 179, 192

YouTube:

ads on, 127, 191–192

affiliate traffic from, 186

for driving traffic, 178, 185–186, 195

followers on, 35

in registration phase, 167

in warming phase, 166